Water-based
Screenprinting

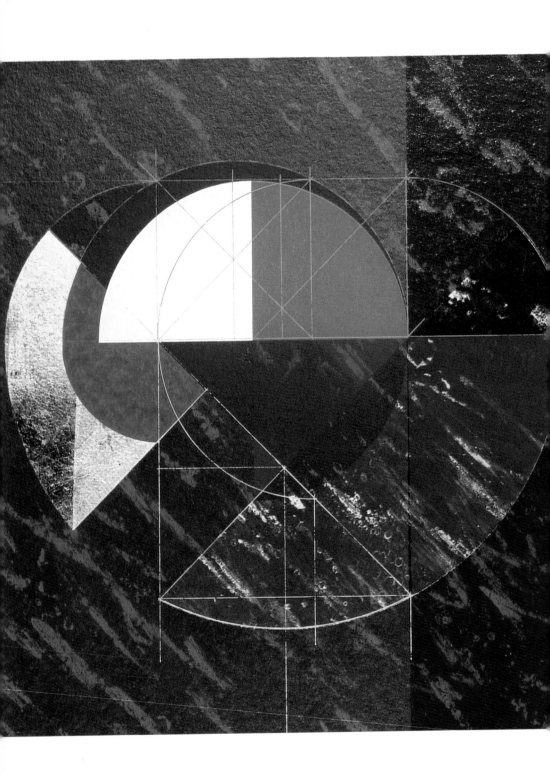

Water-based Screenprinting

STEVE HOSKINS

A & C BLACK • LONDON

First published in Great Britain 2001
A & C Black (Publishers) Limited
37 Soho Square, London W1D 3QZ

ISBN 0-7136-5036-2

A CIP catalogue record for this book is available from the British Library.

Front cover illustration: 'Golden Section 10' by Steve Hoskins.
Back cover illustration: 'Lips and Jugs' by Donna Moran.
Frontispiece: 'Golden Section 11' by Steve Hoskins.

Cover design by Dorothy Moir.

Designed by Janet Jamieson.

Printed in Malaysia by Times Offset (M) Sdn. Bhd.

Publishers note: Printmaking can sometimes involve the use of dangerous substances and sharp tools. Always follow the manufacturer's instructions and store chemicals and inks (clearly labelled) out of the reach of children. All information herein is believed to be accurate, however, neither the author not the publisher can accept any legal liability for errors or omissions.

CONTENTS

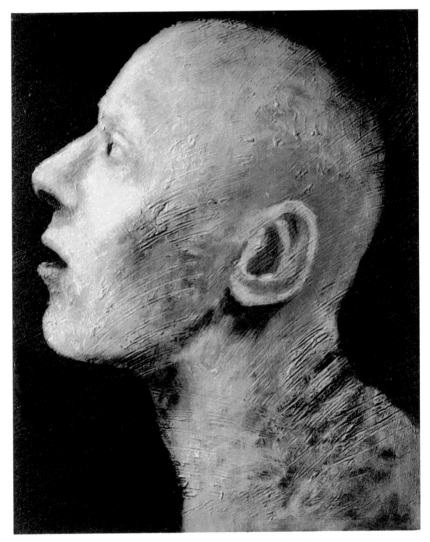

'Head' by John Kirby, UK. Screenprint and woodblock, 74 x 62.5cm, ed. 100.
Photo courtesy of Angela Flowers Gallery.

ACKNOWLEDGEMENTS

My thanks go to John Purcell for his help and advice on paper and for allowing me to use primarily his descriptions on the various types of paper. To Keith Jones for his permission to use his description of scanning into a Macintosh computer, a task I would not have accomplished unaided. Graham Parrish for his patience as a photographer. To all at UWE for their assistance in particular Dave Fortune and Andrew Atkinson but also Richard Anderton, Sarah Bodman and Carinna Parraman. To Rosemary Simmons for her gently chiding corrections and Kevin Petrie for his suggestions. Richard Dixon Wright at Inveresk Paper for allowing us to photograph in the mill. To Libby Lloyd for her assistance and allowing us to photograph at Bath Spa University College. Linda Lambert and Michelle Tiernan at A & C Black for their incredible patience, all who generously lent slides especially Dennis O Neil and Allan Mann for last minute assistance and not least to my wife Barbara for her perseverence.

'Rocket wheel' by Penny Brewill, UK. Screenprint and etching construction,
112 x 76 cm, 1993.
Photo permission the artist.

INTRODUCTION

In just 30 years, screenprinting has become one of the four major tools used by printmakers. Most art school print studios are divided into etching, lithography, relief print and screenprint. It is now difficult to accept that even in 1967 letters were written to the *Guardian* newspaper in England questioning the legitimacy of screenprint as a means of artistic expression.

In the 1990s this means of artistic printmaking was once more under threat. Artists are increasingly concerned with their personal health and the long-term damage that can be caused by some of the chemicals we have taken for granted in the past. Thankfully, at least in the UK, the almost universal adoption of water-based screenprinting means that the decline of screenprinting due to factors of health and unpleasant working conditions has been halted.

In the last decade water-miscible screenprinting inks (commonly and henceforth referred to as water-based inks) have become an established and successful part of printmaking practice. During a visit to Gemini GEL Studios Los Angeles USA in 1995, I saw a suite of David Hockney prints being editioned with TW water-based inks. This provided visual proof that water-based inks could be employed to the highest standards and are comparable, in colour quality, fine line and surface quality to anything that went before. My assumption was if they have been accepted by a major studio as good enough for a blue-chip artist such as Hockney, their quality is no longer an issue.

Of the four largest screenprint editioning studios in London, two have converted to water-based screenprinting, and the other two are slowly accepting that as a younger generation of artist comes through who only know about water-based screenprint, they will have to, at some point, consider change. Art schools in the UK were forced to change because of the Health and Safety at Work Act and the impact of COSHH (control of subtances hazardous to health) regulations. It has helped that water-based inks are considerably cheaper to use. The fact that the cleaning solvent is free – in this case water – is significant in an era of dramatic cuts in funding per student. Screenprinting departments can now at least survive and still function.

Like all new innovations and changes to customary working practices, the transition from solvent to water-based screenprinting ink has not been an easy one for many artists. It is therefore sensible to make clear at the outset of this introduction to a new method of working, that water-based screenprint inks are not identical to solvent-based inks. Therefore, they should not be seen as direct replacements, but rather as something new that has many of the qualities of the old, plus many more advantages. Many aesthetic potentials are now possible which formerly could not have been considered. Of course the lack of noxious smell and greatly reduced financial outlay are also distinct bonuses.

The development of water-based inks suitable for artist's use first began in the late 1980s. For instance, the Swiss company, Lascaux, produced a screenprinting medium for its range of high quality artists' acrylic paints. This was introduced to the UK educational market by the University of the West of England, Bristol. In the USA, although there was more choice with products such as TW Graphics, Union, Hunts Speedball and Createx, the take-up has been slower, primarily due to the relative lack of interest in screenprinting in educational establishments and the dominance of lithography.

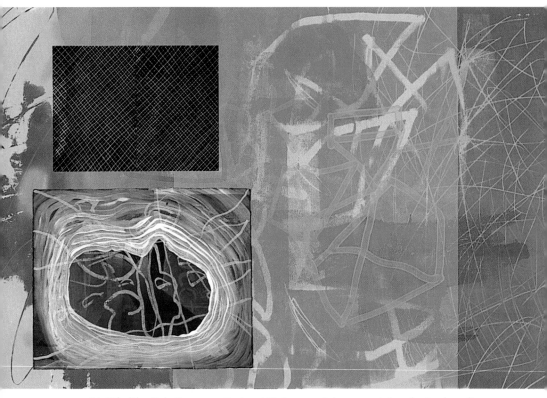

'Untitled' by Dale Deveraux Barker, UK. Screenprint monoprint and mixed media (oil based), 60 x 100cm, 1997. Printed by the artist. Photo permission the artist.

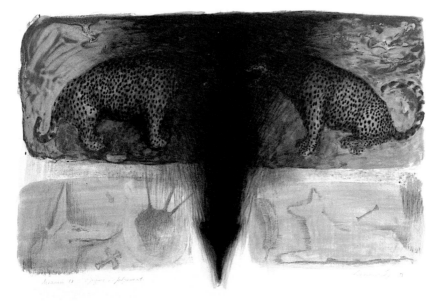

'Arcanum 1, o Jaguar e o Julgamento' by Nogueira Fleury, Brazil. 52.2 x 88.5cm, ed. 40, 1995. Printed and published by Pratt Contemporary Art, Kent, England

It should be acknowledged that a change from solvent-based to water-based was not simply just a matter of changing the brand of ink used. The reality involved the adoption of a completely different process, with only some common elements to the previous system. Water-based screenprinting requires different methods of creating and making stencils, different methods of printing and even changes to the paper printed upon. The hardest factor for most people was the realisation that they had to throw away the personal ink stocks which they had built up, often over many years. As printmakers are often thrifty individuals, to many it seemed like throwing good money away!

It is not surprising, therefore, that the initial acceptance was at first sporadic. People slowly got used to a particular brand of ink and the results, though advantageous to the health and well-being of the individual, were not aesthetically spectacular. I believe this was more a question of mind-set than the failure in quality of the products. It needed a transitional stage, which lasted approximately five years, for one generation of artists to stop making comparisons with the products which had gone before, and a new generation of artists to be introduced to a process of which they had no prior knowledge.

The lack of prior knowledge led to artists asking questions, such as 'will it print a very fine halftone? Which ink do I use? Can I slow or speed its drying?' Demands such as these create new solutions. Users began looking at which products might better suit particular requirements. This in turn has led to a process which can cope with a much more diverse range of aesthetic needs. It is now possible to readily identify a range of products to fulfil specific tasks. For example, Daler Rowney inks for low-cost use in colleges, TW inks for high-quality colour in editioning studios and mediums such as Lascaux for printing fine detailed halftone work. The process of water-based screenprinting has now gained an acceptance and historical context. Artists' editioning studios as diverse as Gemini in Los Angeles and Glasgow Print Studios in Scotland use these products to print

'*The Negotiators*' by Peter Howson, Scotland. 97 x 75cm, ed. 50, 1990. Printed by Glasgow Print Studio. Courtesy of Angela Flowers Gallery.

works by artists such as David Hockney and Peter Howson. Water-based screenprinting is now an integral part of the printmaker's armoury.

If asked to predict a long-term future for screenprint, I do not think the current solution will remain for more than perhaps the next 15 years. This is not to suggest that screenprinting has no future. On the contrary, of all the print processes, by its very nature it has been the most adaptable and I firmly believe it will continue to develop, adapt further, and survive.

To put the above in context, solvent-based screenprinting was unhealthy for the user. The solvents necessary were toxic and consequently carried many health warnings. Therefore, the substitution of solvents with water-based products is an extremely sensible move for the user. However, environmentally, there is probably little to choose between solvent and water-based inks. Both are petrochemical products, plus acrylic resins do not break down easily, to a certain extent, causing disposal problems. The acrylic residue can be filtered from the water system but still must be disposed of in other ways.

As it gets tougher, environmental legislation will at some point force a further reappraisal of these products. Solutions that are healthy for both the user and the environment will eventually come into play. Industry drives the pace of change in this field as in other fields of printmaking. We, as artists, combine the various industrial developments to suit our particular needs, but we can only do this if there is a particular need in industry which will justify the necessary product development costs to create the product in the first place.

What then, is the future for artists and screenprinting? As I have already stated, its very adaptability will cause screenprinting to survive. For example, it is the easiest process to combine both autographic (hand-drawn) and photographic imagery on the same stencil. Already it is possible to buy wide-format films which can have digital inkjeted imagery on one side and hand-drawn mark-making, including delicate washes, on the other. Commercially it is also viable to inkjet straight onto the light-sensitive emulsion coated on a screen. In time, as this technology gets cheaper and the commercial machines enter the second-hand market, this technology will devolve to the artist printmaker. The advent of water-based ink has made the potential for this new expanded medium accessible and more user-friendly.

The field of printmaking itself stands at the crossroads of a new future, as digitally-generated imagery has forced a new debate. Printmaking can be viewed either as an outmoded, outdated means of expression, superseded by the screen-based culture of the new millennium, or it can be viewed as a collaborative communal process that shifts its outlook and perceptions and encompasses the new, without discarding the old.

This begs the question 'Why printmaking?'. Primarily for the screenprinter, there is a quality of surface and tactility sustained from handling a sheet of paper and a means of control of surface and colour offered by no other visual medium. At its best, rich swathes of colour can be applied to the print, which will sit on the surface of the paper and positively glow. The element of touch and feel is also very important to printmakers. It allows an intimacy with small elements, which can have major influences on the final quality and outcome. There is great delight in printing on a delicate handmade sheet of Japanese paper and watching the colour sit on the surface with a positive edge to its boundaries. This intimacy naturally leads to a greater emphasis on how those qualities are conveyed, and if they are not present, the conveying of content will always suffer. Therefore an interest in the technical 'nuts and bolts' of print creation is essential to good printmaking.

This creates the late 20th century printmakers' dilemma; you cannot be a good printmaker without knowledge of technical process, yet in acknowledging technique, you lay yourself open to criticism that technique overrides content. It is a well-known fact that if you put two printmakers in a room with a print, the first question they will ask is 'How's it done?' This is not invariably a denial of content, merely a common ground attempt to form the necessary collaborative dialogue that is essential to function as a printmaker. Finally, therefore, it is that very process of collaboration which printmakers will also cite as integral to the practice of the discipline. It is in the collaborative studios of the last fifty years that some of the best and most innovative work has been created.

It is the marriage of old and new, technique and content, that makes printmaking so exciting at this point in its history. Therefore, though this is primarily a technical handbook, I hope to convey some of the excitement and joy of the practice of screenprinting as a vehicle for conveying ideas.

At this point it is probably wise to define what I mean by the term 'screenprinting'. At its simplest, a screen consists of a frame over which is stretched a fine mesh. The mesh in turn supports the stencil; the stencil is a means of blocking the ink from passing through the screen. Ink is then forced through the open areas of the stencil by means of a squeegee. The squeegee consists of a flexible blade attached to a handle.

This book will deal with each of the stages of making a screenprint, from the preparation of artwork, through to signing, editioning and storing prints.

Chapter 1
SCREENPRINTING HISTORY

This chapter deals with the history of screenprint from its origins at the beginning of the 20th century to its current position for artists at the start of the 21st.

▮ Origins

Many attributions have been made for the origins of the screenprint process, starting as early as the 14th century with the Knights of St John painting *pitch* onto gauze stretched over barrel hoops to print banners. Or, alternatively, the delicate Chinese stencils held together with fine strands of hair. However, each of these is far removed from the process, utilising a frame with a mesh stretched over it to form a screen, a squeegee and a stencil. Even if you accept this definition, there is still much confusion relating to the origins of the screenprinting process. To quote Pat Gilmour in her catalogue to the 'Mechanised Image' exhibition of 1978: 'Despite the fact that it is the only graphic medium to emerge this century, it is as difficult to piece together the early history of screenprinting as to reconstruct 15th century relief printing from the incunabula of the woodcut.'

The defining moments for the birth of screenprint as we know it start either at the end of the 19th century, or at the beginning of the 20th. However, there is no doubt that screenprinting was already firmly established by 1916 when the patent of the Selectasine Company confirmed screenprinting existence prior to the issue of the patent. A survey of all the relevant patents from 1880 to 1916, reveals a patent from 1887 issued to Charles Nelson Jones of Michigan, which has most of the attributes of the screenprinting process. Additionally, in 1907, Samuel Simon of Manchester, England, was granted a patent with many common elements to the 1916 Selectasine patent.

Elinor Noteboom of Orange City, Iowa, has devoted much research to the origins of screenprinting and has traced its beginnings, as a definable process, to the 1887 patent. Her belief is that screenprinting is a direct descendant of the stencil duplicating process, starting with Charles Nelson Jones, through the work of A. B. Dick, who took out a series of patents for stencil duplicating, to the process recognised in the 1916 Selectasine patent. From this point in 1916, screenprint remained a purely commercial process until the 1930s.

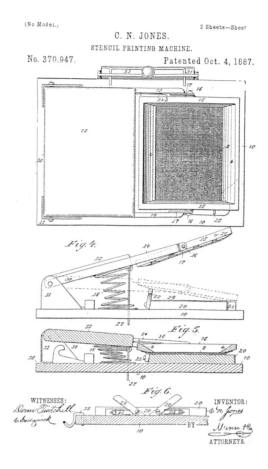

Charles Nelson Jones patent, 1887.

With hindsight it is now feasible to divide the artistic path of the process through the 20th century into a series of stylistic categories. These are closely linked to the manner in which the process was used.

During the Depression of the 1930s the Federal Government in the USA supported artists through a series of projects, run by the Works Progress Administration. Commercial screenprint was adapted to artists' needs and artists such as Harry Gottlieb and Anthony Velonis developed methods of screenprinting by painting an oil-bound resist known as tuche onto the screen, then coating the screen with a water-soluble filler, and when dry, washing the tuche away with solvent. The development of this approach led to a very painterly result with very evident brush marks and a build up of stencil that could only loosely fit together in register. The process of artistic screenprinting at this time became known as *Serigraphy* to differentiate it from the commercial process.

This autographic (worked by hand) method of blocking out the screen in a positive manner with tuche, characterised printmaking of the time both in the US and Europe. Both the characteristics and the results of this style of very painterly mark-making remained the norm for screenprinting until the late 1950s. Whilst the prints of Gottlieb and Velonais (from the 1930s) are frequently reproduced, the work of William Turnball in the UK, who in the 1950s made some of the earliest catalogued artists' screenprints in the UK, is also produced in this manner. As well as being very autographic, Turnbull's prints have a great deal in common with Abstract Expressionism.

In Europe, Luitpold Domberger of Stuttgart was screenprinting for artists throughout the 1950s. He moved the techniques more to the realm of the hand-cut stencil and in collaboration with artists such as Victor Vaserely and Josef Albers, these new methods helped to establish the hard-edged flat colour so frequently associated with screenprinting. The hand-cut films such as Profilm had been around since the late 1920s, but after Domberger it was only in the 1960s and 1970s that they came into frequent use by artists

In the 1960s, screenprinting underwent a technical revolution. New, more sensitive, photographic films came onto the market, and the first thin film paper and board inks began to appear. It was at this point that Pop Art became synonymous with screenprinting. In the UK, Chris Prater at Kelpra (of whom Richard S. Field said in 1973: 'Almost single-handedly Christopher Prater at his Kelpra Studio in London had metamorphosed screenprinting into a fine art') took artists' screenprint to new territory, combining photography, collaged imagery and hand-cut stencils with internationally known artists such as Eduardo Paolozzi, Richard Hamilton, Patrick Caulfield and Jime Dine. In the US artists such as Andy Warhol and Roy Lichtenstein pushed the medium in the same manner. By the end of the 1960s the screenprint process had established itself as a major force within printmaking.

The development of screenprinting now takes an interesting turn. Whilst within the work produced during the 1970s technical virtuosity seems to be the dominant factor, this being the era of the multiple colour blend and hand-rendered photorealistic prints in 70 or more tightly registered printings. For example, I made a lucrative living at the end of this era by producing prints of technical virtuosity, with a concern for colour over content, for the interior decoration market.

At the end of the 1970s, where screenprinting took place was beginning to change. The American dominance of the medium began to wane, and in the USA lithography and etching became the primary media after the 1970s. In the UK screenprint remained a major influence along with etching, and lithography had less prominence.

The 1980s are perhaps characterised by the monoprint. In the UK the two major studios in London were Chris Betambeau and Bob Saitch's Advanced Graphics and Brad Faine's Coriander Studios. Brad Faine, working with Bruce Maclean, even began to dispense with the screen and produced a series of large monoprints with Maclean, where, for the majority of the prints, the ink had been poured directly onto the paper and then pulled across its surface with the squeegee. Advance Graphics, on the other hand, began to combine screenprint with woodblock printings on top to create the added texture which characterised their work with John Walker and Albert Irvine.

Current screenprinting

Screenprint became a choice as a method of production for the artist for a number of reasons: primarily its speed, colour qualities, ability to print on a number of differing substrates, and its capacity to print large, flat, open areas of colour. Now new factors have come into play with water-based inks, one of which is the ability to produce delicate wash marks akin to lithography. This is as much due to developments in stencil making as the introduction of water-based ink and the ability to print much finer half-tone photographic renditions which have been made possible by the slower drying properties of some of the new inks. Examples of this may be seen in the Nogueira Fleury print (see p. 11) produced by Pratt Contemporary Art. These large prints are in vibrant colour yet with delicate wash structures built up in many layers.

In recent years, as printmakers in general have sought to expand the boundaries of the discipline, screenprint has been ideally placed to meet those new demands. More artists than ever wish to print on different surfaces and substrates. This mirrors screenprinting's industrial expansion of the last 20 years.

Therefore, users of screenprint often integrate more than one process or discipline. In California, Gemini GEL (one of America's primary print studios) combines screenprint with lithography when printing for David Hockney. The recent 'Hot off the Press' show dealing with printed ceramics, shows renewed interest in combining print and ceramics. At the University of the West of England, we have developed a water-based screenprinted ceramic transfer system, which can be seen demonstrated in the work of Dr Kevin Petrie (see p. 20) the researcher in this area.

The artist's book is another area demonstrating the expanding borders of screenprint. In the past, text was thought not suitable to be screenprinted. Now with computer typesetting and laser print transparency films, it is common to output the text and print it with a water-based ink that is slow to dry in the screen, thus enabling crisp printed text to be maintained with no drying in of the screen.

Industrial uses

Screenprinting has become a serious industrial force in the last two decades. From the non-unionised poor relation of the print industry, it

'Revelation II' by Ana Maria Pacheco, Brazil. Screenprint, 1565 x 1175mm, edition of 15, 1993. Printed and published by Pratt Contemporary Art, Kent, UK.

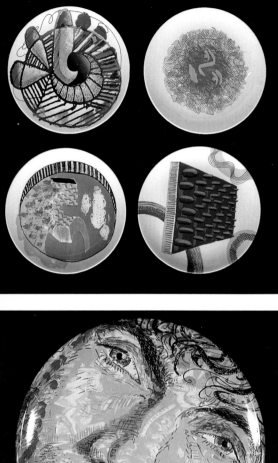

has expanded to quietly dominate the non-paper and board sector of the market. A diverse range of products, from the heated rear window of your car through to the sensor used to test whether you have diabetes, all are screen-printed. The major areas of industrial print are graphics and point of sale, industrial processes, textiles and garment printing, glass and ceramics, electronics including circuit boards and biomedical equipment. Wide-format digital print has moved into some of the traditional commercial screen-print territory, particularly in the area of short runs and trial proofs. In response, commercial screen-printing has just moved on and captured new territory. For example, every CD is now screen-printed directly onto its surface.

Screenprinting has evolved and adapted to meet the changing market more than any other print process, perhaps because it is fundamentally the simplest. For the artist, this constant adaptation to meet a particular need means there are always new developments in industry, which will in time filter down to be capitalised and adapted by the printmaking fraternity.

Top: *'Four plates'* by Kevin Petrie, UK. Screenprinted on-glaze ceramic transfer, 25cm diameter, 1998.

Above: *'Handsome dish'* by Kevin Petrie, UK. Screenprinted on-glaze ceramic transfer, 30cm diameter, 1997. Photos courtesy of the artist.

Chapter 2

ARTWORK PREPARATION

This chapter deals with translating your original idea into a format from which you can make stencils. It covers methods of hand-drawing suitable artwork and photographically preparing artwork both from the computer and in the traditional photographic manner.

This chapter assumes all artwork will be prepared before making the screen. The old methods, including preparing a stencil by painting directly on the screen, are no longer applicable. Even in solvent-based screenprinting, this method has not been prevalent for many years. Using water-based inks, direct stencil preparation on the screen is extremely limited.

Stencils may be hand-drawn on a variety of materials and photo-polymer emulsions are now so sensitive that detail can be produced from lightly drawn marks that previously would have been impossible to render. This is perhaps a good point to explain the difference between the terms autographic and photographic stencils.

Autographic means drawn by hand and covers any form of artwork which is drawn, painted or cut by hand. If this artwork is subsequently dealt with by a photographic process, it would still be termed autographic.

Photographic in this context means any artwork that is created solely by photography and for expediency in this book anything that is generated or captured by computer.

Hand-rendered stencils (autographic)

Paper masks

The simplest form of stencil is made from paper. These are used primarily if resources are limited or you need to print a few trial prints of simple shapes. Paper stencils can be cut and placed under the screen. They are created by drawing or tracing the image onto the sheet of paper to be used as a stencil, then cutting away with a very sharp knife all the parts you wish to print (see illustration on p. 22). The best type of paper for this is probably greaseproof paper. It is cheap and will last for approximately ten prints. Other papers such as newsprint and copy paper can be used but will only last for a very few prints.

Cutting paper stencils. Use a sharp scalpel to give a crisp edge.

Paper masks are adhered to the screen with small blobs of printing medium.

First place the drawing on the bed of the press, then lay the paper stencil in position on the drawing – this will make sure all the bits of stencil print in the correct place – having masked a generous border around the edges so that there is enough room for the squeegee to print properly. (See Chapter Three on Screen preparation.) Then lower the screen gently onto the paper and tack the paper in place with a few blobs of printing ink or clear printing base.

Knife-cut films

Knife-cut films are used when simple solid shapes with crisp edges are needed. The traditional knife-cut films which are adhered directly to the screen are not suitable for water-based screenprinting. Therefore only red photographic masking films, such as Amberlith and Rubylith are used. The purpose of these films is to block the light from the direct emulsions currently used. These are used when crisp-edged stencils are required or when a mask for a photographic stencil is needed to fit with great accuracy. They come as a red/orange plastic coating attached to a transparent polyester backing sheet. The red coating is cut with a sharp knife or scalpel taking care not to cut through the plastic backing sheet. Then unwanted areas of film are peeled away. This leaves the shapes you wish to print as patches of red supported by the film backing. The red colouring is more effective than the orange at blocking the ultra-violet light emitted by the light sources which are used to harden the direct emulsions.

Magic tape

This is the form of Sellotape or Scotch Tape, which is manufactured for temporary invisible repairs to paper which can then be photocopied, or for marking objects, as it can be drawn upon with ink. It is translucent in appearance. In screenprinting it can be used, if applied to the uppermost

Knife cut films. Care must be taken not to cut through the plastic support backing.

Magic tape. Note that this temporary stencil has to be rubbed down very firmly on a dry screen in order for it to work.

side of a dry screen and rubbed down hard with a finger, to make sure all the surface of the tape is adhered to the screen. If treated with care, this tape makes a good temporary stencil and can also be used to mask parts of stencils not currently in use.

Drafting films

These films are used for hand-drawn line work or when you have simple shapes or bold drawing. They are becoming superseded by films such as True Grain and Mark Resist. They commonly have a matt and a shiny side. All drawing takes place on the matt side. They are usually found under trade names such as Kodatrace or Permatrace. Single matt means one side only may be drawn upon (the other side is shiny). Double matt means both sides can be drawn upon. They will accept a limited variety of drawing materials: Rotring film ink, chinagraph pencil, litho crayons and photopaque are the most common. Due to the smooth matt surface, care has to be taken to use only drawing materials that adhere well to the surface and which will create a strong dense mark.

Textured films (*True Grain*)

These are an extension of drafting films and are made of polyester with a fine-textured (grainy) surface; this grainy surface retains small particles of pigment, thus creating a very wide range of printable marks. These films are primarily manufactured for pressure-sensitive washable or wipe-clean key pads, such as tills in butchers' shops, and are found under the trade names of True Grain, Mark Resist or Lexan. They come in a number of different grain surfaces, but the former two tend to be finer than Lexan. The beauty of these products is that, because of the textured surface, they create a very fine random dot structure just by drawing on them. This allows an infinite variety of marks that can be made with any number of

ARTWORK PREPARATION

drawing materials. The possible aesthetic effect varies from very fine tonal washes which are almost indistinguishable from a lithographic mark, through delicate pencil drawing, to dense black solids drawn with acrylic paint (see illustration).

Alternative photostencils

Tissue and tracing paper can be used as drafting films for making photostencils; they are cheap alternatives that render well for single colour printing. These are also acceptable for multiple colour printing that does not have to fit in register. They can be drawn on with soft pencil, chinagraph and litho crayons. Ink tends to make them cockle and curl up.

On the right is drafting film and on the left is textured film/true grain. Both types are shown with the type of mark best suited to each (see chart on p. 25).

On the left is tracing paper and on the right is tissue paper. With care, a mapping pen and soft pencil may be used on tracing paper.

Test sheet of drawing marks. Note the rubbing taken from a piece of lace in the bottom left-hand corner.

Set of hand-drawn marks and how they print

Above: textured drafting film original

Graphite stick

Dip pen using
Staedtler ink

Ink with
methylated
spirits

Ink with
sandpaper
scratches

Chinagraph
pencil

Chinagraph
pencil

Gouache with
knife scratches

Ink with
Vaseline
(petroleum
jelly) resist

Above: screenprinted result

Drawing materials

Working onto a plastic support film such as True Grain or drafting film, rather than directly onto the screen, has a number of advantages. Not least is the number of materials one can actually use to draw with. Other advantages include the ability to remake the same stencil if you lose your screen or something disastrous happens to it, plus the ability to use the drawn artwork to line up the paper when printing (see Chapter Six).

Chinagraph pencil and litho crayons

These will work on drafting film, textured films and also tracing paper. They are at their best if a bold, very wide crayon-type mark is required. When using, keep a sharp knife handy, as the softer litho crayons need to be sharpened frequently. A good solid black line comes up the best with these tools. Once the use of chinagraph pencils is mastered, this method can produce a wide variety of marks and quite subtle effects, especially if used in combination with a scalpel to scratch back into the marks created.

Pencils

Very soft pencils will work on drafting film, textured film and tracing paper. The harder the pencil, the poorer the result, though textured films are capable of picking up extremely subtle marks.

Acrylic paint

This will work very well on drafting film and textured films as an opaque blocking medium. If watered down, watercolour wash effects can be achieved.

Tuche and drawing ink washes

Tuche is a greasy pigmented drawing stick used by lithographic print-makers. It is dissolved in water to create an ink that can be painted. Alternatively, Faber Castell or Rotring drawing inks thinned with water may be used. Each of these will create different effects.

This technique really only works on the textured films like true grain and mark resist. Care has to be taken that the stencils are not painted too thinly. A very pale piece of artwork means a drastic reappraisal of exposure time. The resultant under-exposure can lead to stencils breaking down far too readily.

Biro, fine liners and felt-tip pens

None of these work very well. Occasionally it is possible to find one that works, but as a general rule avoid all of the above; they tend not to make a dense enough mark.

Methylated spirit (and Vaseline)

Both make interesting effects when used in combination with the tuche wash effects onto textured films. (See previous page for examples.)

Copy toner

I mention this primarily as it is gives excellent wash effects. Copy toner is the thermoplastic fine powder used for photocopiers. **It is carcinogenic and not recommended for general use. Ensure good health and safety precautions are in place.** If used with methylated spirit it produces very delicate washes on True Grain-type films. These washes are unstable so ensure that the film and toner is handled very carefully.

The chart below gives a list of materials and the surfaces which they may be used upon.

	tracing paper	drafting film	textured film
Pencil	✓	✓	✓
Chinagraph	✓	✓	✓
Litho crayon	✓	✓	✓
Tuche washes	✗	✗	✓
Acrylic paint	✗	✗	✓
Rotring ink	✗	✓	✓
Drawing ink	✗	✗	✓
Faber castell Ink	✗	✓	✓
Biro	✗	✗	✗
Meths	✗	✗	✓
Copy toner	✗	✓	✓
Lip balm	✗	✗	✓

Making multiple separations

This is how a multiple colour print is made. Each colour has to be separated out and an individual black artwork stencil is made for each colour.

The simplest method of registering multiple stencils is to draw up a master sheet of the image in line only, and then in the four corners draw four sets of crosses. As each individual stencil is placed on top in register, mark the four corners with the set of crosses, thus enabling each sheet to be placed back in exactly the same position and capable of being registered with all the other stencils.

When drawing stencils, it must be noted that a degree of overlap must be built into each stencil; in industry this is called the *trap*. It is not possible, given the variations in screen and paper stretch, to guarantee a perfect fit when printing. Therefore it is necessary to build in a small degree of overlap for every stencil.

The other alternative is to use a pin bar registration system, as used in industry. This enables extremely accurate registration as well as the ability to make multiple exposures when making complicated stencils. Each stencil is punched with the pin register punch (see overleaf) then a register bar is attached to the master drawing and the stencils aligned onto the register bar.

The use of the pin bar system does allow the making of multiple expo-sures, for example, if one desires a patch of texture in the middle of a perfectly round circle. First, the stencil with patch of texture is exposed for the normal exposure time. The first stencil is then replaced with a stencil of a circle that blocks the UV light. This stencil is then also exposed for the normal exposure. When the screen is washed out, the result will print as a crisp round circle with a patch of texture running up to its edges but not beyond.

1. Multiple exposure using a pin register bar. Pin register punch for accurately punching registration holes and aligning the two stencils onto the pin register bar.

2. The first stencil and the pin register bar taped to the screen in register.

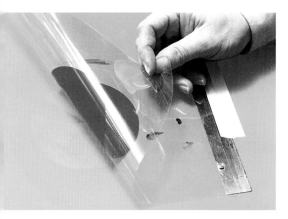

3. The second stencil and the pin register bar taped to the screen in register.

4. The two stencils, the pin register bar and the printed result.

'Edo Kite II' by Steve Hoskins, UK. Screenprint on Japanese paper with gloss fibre rod, 1120 x 1450 mm. Finished print from registration process, 1999.

Photographic stencils

Traditional graphic arts films

Traditionally, photostencils were made for screenprint using a graphic arts film such as Litex. These films were specifically made for the reprographics industry to make photographic film positives and negatives in large sizes using a copy camera, which could then be transferred to a light-sensitive lithographic plate or sensitised screen. In recent years, this photographic film output has been computer-generated. The films use a two-part developer and were processed and fixed as a normal black and white photographic paper print. A 35mm or larger-format negative is placed into the film carrying head in an enlarger and projected onto the sheet of film attached to the baseboard. When developed, a film positive is produced. To surmount the difficulties of applying a halftone to the resultant film positive, the grain of the 35mm negative is often used. If a high-contrast film, such as recording film or uprated HP5 (to 800 or 1200 ASA), is used and developed in a developer such as HC110, which gives a crisper profile to the grain, a halftone becomes unnecessary.

This technique has the capability of producing several positives of varying densities (one under-exposed, one normal density, one over-exposed) from one negative, without incurring an interference pattern. The results when printed lead to an appearance of more solid rendering. This technique is known as posterisation (see Tim Mara, Thames & Hudson). Dry-process graphic arts films, such as CPN and CPF, can also be used in this manner.

Due to the almost total acceptance by the reprographic industry of computer generation and digital film output, these films and the technology are becoming increasingly difficult to obtain. However, for artists, these films in combination with an enlarger or copy camera still offer a range of techniques unobtainable elsewhere. Already they are best obtained from a specialist supplier of alternative photographic materials. (See the list of suppliers on p. 107.)

Computer generation

This is now the most common method of generating photographic stencils for screenprinting. At its simplest level, all that is necessary is a scanner, a PC or Mac, a laser printer, plus a programme such as Photoshop.

Scanning

Scanning is useful not just for copying photographs and drawings in order to transfer them to film output with a halftone, but also can be used with actual objects and artefacts. Even three-dimensional objects will fit under most scanners if the depth of the object is not to great.

To scan an image is almost as simple as doing a photocopy. Use the scanning software installed on your computer – usually Photoshop, open the scanning programme, and then acquire the scanner. This is normally found under the file command in the menu. It will normally say 'Get picture', if you click on 'get picture', the command to acquire should appear, having established communication between the computer and the scanner. Put the artwork or object to be scanned face down on the scanner bed and lower the lid. If scanning a three-dimensional object, cover with a white cloth to block out the light. Next define the parameters within the window on screen. Are you scanning in colour? If so, select RGB colour. Next select the resolution: 150 dpi (this is explained in greater detail later). Choose a size. 100% is fine, as any adjustments to the magnification are best made at a later stage. Besides, magnifying the image at this stage slows the scanning operation down to hibernating tortoise pace. Once all these parameters are defined, then scanning can commence. First preview the image, this establishes the position of the picture on the scanner bed. Next encapsulate the image with the active rectangle on the representation of the scanner bed, this saves wasting unnecessary computer space and memory. Finally, hit the scan button. You can then save your digitally encoded scan to the desired place in the documents folder.

Adobe Photoshop ™

Adobe Photoshop is used by most of the major newspapers, magazines and design houses to originate or creatively alter images to suit their purposes. When Photoshop has been started by double clicking on the icon in the Photoshop folder, the image can be opened. Click on File – Open, then the name of your image in the hierarchical list is now displayed. Once the image has appeared on the screen it can be manipulated to satisfy your creative instincts. Colours can be adjusted, but it is important to remember that you are viewing the picture on a monitor screen; luminosity, hue and saturation of the colours are all different from the original. The image is being viewed by transmitted light from three electron guns at the back of the monitor cathode ray tube, rather than reflected from a piece of paper by whatever light source you happen to find yourself in. In general the rule is to use the original as your guide, not the screen, as no two monitors present an image in exactly the same colours. Just take a look at the array of televisions in a store. The scope of Photoshop is enormous; much too comprehensive to be explained within this brief précis. Suffice it to say that if you think of what you want it to do, then Photoshop will more than likely enable you to do it.

How colour separations work

Once the picture has been suitably manipulated to your creative satisfaction, then it is time to decide on the parameters needed to produce your image in print. Computer specialists use acronyms such as 'dpi' or 'lpi' when they are talking about printing from their computer. Dpi means dots per inch, or the resolution of the computer image. Computers make up images from pixels; dpi is the expression of the number of those pixels to the square inch. The greater the number of pixels, the finer the resolution of the picture. The penalty to be paid is that the higher the resolution, then the greater the storage space needed on your hard drive or disk. Another factor to be considered before deciding on the resolution of your image is the resolution of the output device or printer. For example, let us assume we are using a 600 dpi laser printer. It is therefore reasonable to assume that there is nothing to be gained by scanning at a resolution greater than the resolution of the output device, in this case the laser printer. In practice, a resolution of half that of the printer is perfectly acceptable. Even less will suffice; a resolution of 150 dpi will be adequate for silk screen, as long as the final image size remains the same as the scanned image size.

The reason for this becomes clear with the explanation of the other acronym 'lpi' or lines (of halftone dots) per inch. The easiest way to explain this state of affairs is to revert to monochrome for the moment.

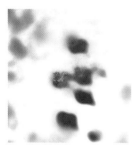
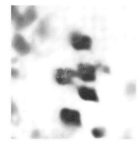

Unconverted scan shown as dpi (dots per inch).

100 lpi. Scan converted to Halftone lines per inch.

50 lpi. This size of dot is easily screenprinted.

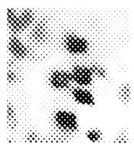
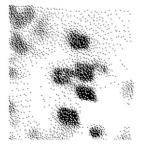

25 lpi. Note at this scale it is easy to see the varying size of dot.

100 dpi bitmap. Note all the dots are of a uniform size.

When you see a greyscale (a range of tones from black to white) photograph reproduced in a publication on a page with some black text, there is only black ink on that page; yet the photograph appears to have a complete tonal range from black, through various shades of grey, to white. This is achieved by breaking the picture up into lines of dots of varying sizes. The black ink interacts with the surrounding white paper to give an optical illusion of grey. The bigger, and therefore closer together, the black dots are, the darker the image will appear when viewed at a reasonable viewing distance. Consequently the smaller, and further apart the black dots are, the lighter grey they will appear to be. Take this a stage further and put cyan, magenta, yellow and black lines of halftone dots on top of one another at varying angles and you create a full colour spectrum optical illusion using only four colours.

The final image is then saved as a CMYK image in the mode menu in Photoshop. This means that the image is broken down into four channels or colour separations. CMYK stands for cyan, magenta, yellow and keyline, or black. These are the four-colour process printing primary colours, the theory is that as pure colours cyan, magenta and yellow, when combined together, make up black. But in practice they do not; so black is added to make up for any shortfalls of dark tone. Each of the printing primaries is then broken up into a series of lines of dots, or lpi, (also called a halftone), and a separation made for each colour. So if the image contains lots of yellow, for instance, then the yellow separation will have lots of dots on it. Or if the image is composed of a predominance of blue, then the cyan and magenta separations will be heavily dotted, as cyan and magenta make up blue.

'Red Andalucia' by Kristian Krokfors, Finland. 55 x 92.4cm, ed. 55, printed by Pratt Comtemporary Art, 1999.
Photo courtesy Pratt Contemporary Art, Kent, England.

ARTWORK PREPARATION

Halftone screening

At this stage it is important to say a few words about the use of halftones in screenprinting. To recap on what we have covered so far, halftones in printing are used to render tone from black to white. Images of continuous tone in photography can be represented by breaking the structure into dots. A mid-tone grey consists of 50% white dots and 50% black dots; black is achieved with solid black dots and white with no dots. In reality, this is impossible to achieve, for screenprinting 10% dots in the white and 85% in the black is the accepted norm. (See table below.)

The reason for this is based on the relationship of the halftone dot and the mesh structure of the screen. To be supported, i.e. stuck to the screen mesh, the smallest dot (which is a dot from the blackest area) needs to be adhered to at least three strands of mesh. Conversely, the smallest hole needs to not fall across a strand of mesh in order to be printable. It should be noted that the dots below 50% (the highlights in the positive) will be the lower percentage opening on the stencil, and all the dots above 50% (the shadows) will be the largest percentage of open area on the stencil. For more accurate guidance of which halftone ranges are suitable for each mesh count, and the percentage of tonal range that is printable from that mesh, please refer to the table below.

Halftone (cm/in)	Mesh count/ thread diameter UK	USA	Highlight %	Shadow %
24 (60)	20.34	305	10	90
	120.40	305	12	88
34 (86)	140.31	355	12	88
	140.34	355	14	85
	150.31	380	14	85
	150.34	380	14	85
40 (100)	150.31	380	12	80
	150.34	380	12	80
	165.31	420	12	80
	165.34	420	12	80

Moiré

Due to the increased use of direct stencil systems by artists, moiré has become a factor to be dealt with. The crossing of two gridded structures can produce an interference pattern and unattractive effect similar to that seen in watered silk, which is referred to as moiré silk, hence the use of the term.

It is possible to minimise the effect in the following ways. Using a finer mesh that is not an exact mathematical ratio to the halftone ruling for

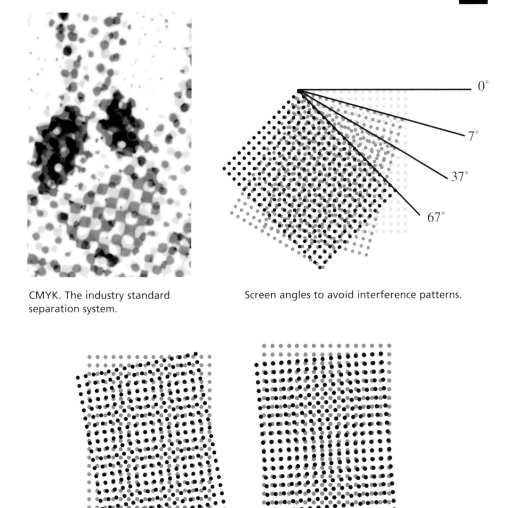

CMYK. The industry standard separation system.

Screen angles to avoid interference patterns.

Examples of a Moiré interference structure.

example, with a 100 lpi use a 145 mesh screen rather than a 150 or conversely, use 93 or 97 lpi with a 150 mesh screen.

If feasible, try using a direct/indirect stencil. This is a light-sensitive emulsion precoated on a plastic support backing (Cappilex is the most common) which is adhered to the mesh and dried before exposure. The profile of the stencil is less affected by the screen mesh and supplies what is known as good mesh bridging. A single coat of direct emulsion is likely to enhance the moiré effect. This is due to the profile of the coating closely matching the shape of the weave, and therefore making it more susceptible to moiré.

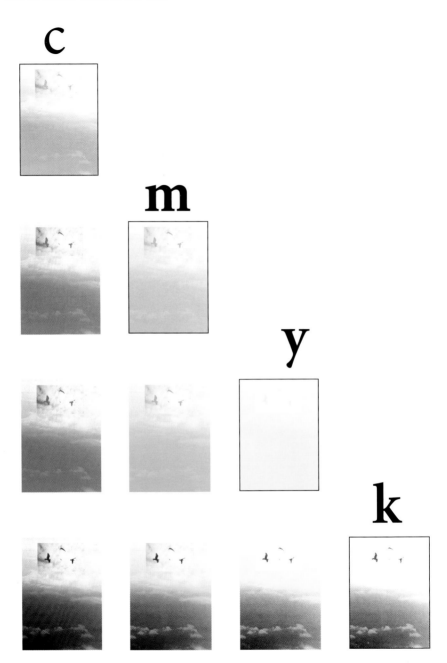

A full set of progressive printings. The left hand column shows the printing steps to reach the full CMYK.

Care should be taken to attach the stencils to the screen at the correct angles, assuming the weave of the screen is taken as the angles 0° and 90° the artwork needs to be generated with a halftone angle, that when placed on the screen will not interfere with these two angles on the mesh. It is therefore common sense not to generate films with an angle of 0° and 90° because the dots will run parallel to the threads. 45° is also not used as the elliptical dot shape has a similar profile to the open areas of the weave and fine detail can be lost. For each colour printing it is also preferable to keep an angle of 30° between each colour in order to create an optimum printed dot pattern. The colours that are lightest, and least likely to show evidence of an interference structure, are assigned angles closest to those of the mesh, in this case yellow and keyline (black). The recommended angles for the least interference are:

Black 7°   Magenta 37°   Cyan 67°   Yellow 97°

The screen can be marked in pencil by drawing first on the screen the right angles created by the weave. This is done, after cleaning and degreasing, on a dry screen, before coating with emulsion; pencil marks will usually show up after coating. At this point, if your screen is badly stretched this weave structure may not be in a straight line. The answer is to have screens professionally stretched. If the correct angles have been generated by the computer and a halftone ruling has ben created that does not interfere with the mesh count. It should be a simple matter to align the film stencils along the horizontal lines marked on the screen and attached with small pieces of magic tape after the screen has been coated and dried. If the above rules are followed, moiré can normally be kept to a minimum.

If it is impractical to mark each screen before each coating, and exposure takes place, the usual practical solution means holding each film against the mesh, viewing the film and the mesh against the light and turning the film until the least amount of moiré is noticed. The screen is then lightly marked in pencil where the edges of the film can be aligned and taped to the screen with Magic Tape before exposure. Speed is of the essence if this procedure is undertaken in daylight with a freshly coated sensitive screen.

Printing out halftone separation films from Photoshop

Having scanned in the artwork and converted it to CMYK, the means of printing out separations are as follows:

Go to 'Page Set-up' under the 'File' menu
Select 'Screen'
De-select 'Use Printers Default Screens' (this will automatically open the commands for setting the screen ruling for the cyan).

Under Frequency	Specify the lines per inch output. This is your halftone screen resolution (for a 120 screen an average would be 47 lpi).

ARTWORK PREPARATION

Under Angle	for cyan type in 67°
Under Shape	Select Ellipse

Select magenta
Under Frequency	Specify the lines per inch output. 47 lpi.
Under Angle	for magenta type in 37°
Under Shape	Check Ellipse is selected

Select yellow
Under Frequency	Specify the lines per inch output. 47 lpi.
Under Angle	for yellow type in 97°
Under Shape	Check Ellipse is selected

Select black
Under Frequency	Specify the lines per inch output. 47 lpi.
Under Angle	for Black type in 7°
Under Shape	Check Ellipse is selected

Click OK
Select Registration Marks, Calibration bars (if available) and Labels.
This last box is very important as otherwise it can be very difficult to tell
the separations apart. This individually labels the cyan, magenta, yellow
and black films. Registration is crucial for correctly aligning the four
separations whilst printing so that the correct colour balance and
appearance is maintained, for details on registration see Chapter Six,
Printing, on page 78.

Laser copy films
These films come under a variety of brand names such as Folex laser film
matt. They are stable polyester films capable of withstanding the heat from
a laser printer or photocopier without distortion. A4 and A3 are the most
common sizes. For basic text output or simple halftone imagery, these
are by far the cheapest way of producing a stencil. It is quite possible to
produce a four-colour separation set with these films which will print in
register. It can be hard to work out the correct screen angle on the screen
to reduce the effect of moiré, as they are translucent rather than
transparent, and therefore it is hard to see the interference structure
through the stencil and mesh together.

Use of a commercial reprographics bureau
For larger more accurate output, it is often cost effective to use the
services of a bureau. These are found in the Yellow Pages under
Typesetters' or Printers' Services. A bureau specialises in producing the
highest-quality film output for printers from computer artwork. Care
should be taken when specifying output to them. It is important to
remember that most bureaux work for lithographers who need negative

artwork. **Screen-printers need positives**. The correct method of specifying for screenprint is to ask for right-reading film positives, emulsion side up. This means that when viewed normally, the film positive has text that reads the correct way round and the layer of film emulsion is on the topmost side. Make sure, when giving disks to bureaux, that you have checked they use the same type of disks as you do, the same versions of the programmes you have used, and that you have included the original scanned files (TIFF or EPS) of any scans you have used in the final version, and finally for any fonts that you have used include the suitcases. This may sound complicated, but it avoids expensive mistakes and endless return trips to sort out problems.

This form of artwork will give the most accurate rendition to your stencil. As we have seen, the resolution of the Laser Printer is 600 dpi. The resolution of an Imagesetter, used by most bureaux, will be in the region of 3,600dpi. This will only have real effect for high-quality line artwork.

'*Black*' by Libby Lloyd, UK. 51 x 51cm, 1998. Artwork based on magnified four colour separation set. Photo courtesy of the artist.

Chapter 3

SCREENS AND STENCILS

This chapter deals with types of screen frame, mesh, stencil coatings and the preparation of screens from coating through exposure to preparing the screen for printing, then how to clean and de-grease screens.

Screens

At its simplest, a screen consists of a frame over which is stretched a fine mesh. The mesh in turn supports the stencil. Ink is then forced through the stencil by means of a squeegee.

Frames

Screen frames can be made from wood, steel or aluminium. Wood will warp, expand and shrink, dependent on atmospheric conditions. It also retains water, thus taking longer to dry than metal. Steel frames will last longer, but have fallen out of favour, due to their heavy weight and tendency to rust. For most purposes I recommend aluminium frames due to their light weight and ease of use. If working to a tight budget, it is possible to buy packs of pre-stretched wooden or MDF (multi density fibred) frames.

The cheapest frames are manufactured from wood. Hardwoods such as beech, cedar and piranha pine are the best to use. The joints should have mortise and tenon or dovetail joints. Any form of simpler jointing will come apart in a very short time. Care must be taken that the corners and outer edges of the frames are rounded so that splinters or rough edges do not damage the mesh when stretching. Once made, the frames should be varnished before stretching, to prevent water retention.

Aluminium frames are the most popular, due to their light weight. Also, they are less prone to warping than wooden frames and their cost has decreased in recent years due to their popularity. They have also gained in popularity for artist's use, as it is now far more common to have frames

Opposite: *'Palace of everyones prosperity'* by Alexander Brodsky, Russia. Screenprint on Somerset paper, 102 x 74cm, 1998. Printed by Dennis O Neil at Hand Print Workshop International, Alexandria, Virginia, USA. Photo courtesy of Hand Print Workshop.

commercially stretched rather than stretching by hand. It is advisable that aluminium frames are checked on a regular basis for sharp edges and any leaks in the welds which allow water into the frame.

When deciding on a size of frame, the inside measurement of the frame must always allow for at least a 13cm (5in.) border around the size of image you are using. This is to allow room for the ink and squeegee, otherwise there is not enough room to use them properly. It also ensures that you will be able to apply an even pressure with the squeegee across the whole surface of the image. If the stencil is too close to the frame, it is sometimes not possible to exert enough pressure to enable that portion of the image near the frame to print.

Screen borders. Note the generous gap between the edge of the screen and the start of the stencil.

Mesh

With water-based inks, mesh has a greater role to play. As the solvent for the inks is water, a minimum deposit is required to prevent undue expansion of the paper; opposed to this, most water-based inks use pigment in suspension, thus the aim is for a heavy deposit to increase colour intensity. Mesh count therefore becomes more specific to the brand of ink, and to my knowledge there are now at least 28 different inks available. The pigment of some of the cheaper brands is not as finely ground as that in some of the more expensive brands, so will not go through the finest meshes easily. However, some general rules apply.

Traditionally, there are two mesh thread diameter descriptions: t and hd (t = standard, hd = heavy duty), which are interpreted differently by each manufacturer. More recently, thread diameter measured in microns is being introduced as a standard description. So meshes are now denoted in two ways: (a) a figure (number of threads per centimetre) and a letter (diameter of thread) and (b) a pair of figures (threads per centimetre and diameter in microns).

The accepted norm for all solvent-based screenprinting inks in mesh counts was 90t for general printing and 110-120t for fine detail. With water-based inks, use 120t (120.34) meshes for most printing, up to 150t

(150.34) for fine halftones and, for a solid background that needs strong colour, 90*t* (90.40) (or for some manufacturers 90.48), but be prepared with these coarser meshes for some cockling or paper expansion, as the coarser the mesh the more water deposited on the paper, and hence more cockling. With the use of direct emulsions it is now more important to have screens stretched tightly and evenly, 14 Newtons is average for a 120*t* screen (a Newton is the Si unit of force used to measure tension). A tension meter for measuring the tension of the mesh is available from large commercial suppliers of screenprinting products. It is only of use when checking the tension of screens for printing very tight-registration halftones, or if stretching a large number of screens yourself. Gauging of screen tension for almost all purposes can be done adequately by feel.

Monofilament polyester meshes, which have replaced all other types for most uses, come in several forms. Plain weave is fine for all printmaking uses. The newest high modulus screens stretched to very high tensions (up to 40 Newtons) are too new yet for general use as the extra expense outweighs any small gains in accuracy. Twill and calendered meshes are probably not applicable for most printmaking as they are more expensive, and offer no advantages. The recommended meshes, combined with a very sharp squeegee and the correct amount of snap whilst printing, reduce

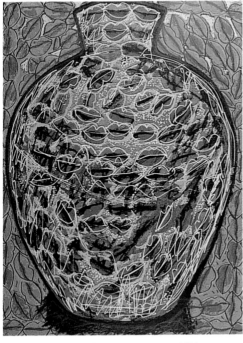

'*My New Portrait*' by Donna Moran, USA. Water-based screenprint, 43 x 36cm.

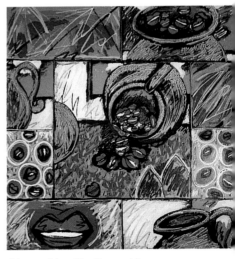

'*Lips and Jugs*' by Donna Moran, USA. Water-based silkscreen, 48 x 48cm.

surface tension to a minimum, allowing a controlled quantity of ink and therefore water onto the paper. If you use direct emulsions, it also costs far less to coat a screen with tight mesh, as you can obtain a much thinner deposit. Orange dyed meshes stop the light from being reflected and scattered when using direct coatings and this is important for fine detail and halftones. They are known as anti-halation meshes.

Finally, it is usually cheaper to have screens stretched professionally, than it is to buy the mesh and do it yourself.

Stencils

Stencils now fall into several categories: firstly, paper (see Chapter Two, Artwork preparation), then hand-painted filler directly painted on the screen and water-soluble polymer coatings on a plastic backing which can be cut with a knife and adhered to the screen with a damp sponge. Apart from paper, these last two are no longer applicable to water-based screenprinting.

The next set of stencils are all light-sensitive polymers generically known as photographic stencils. These come as direct, the most popular of which are liquid emulsions, which are coated directly onto the screen, dried and then exposed to ultra-violet light which hardens the emulsion. The film positive artwork is placed between the screen and the ultra-violet light source, thus blocking the light from the emulsion, and enabling the stencil to be created. After exposure, the softer parts of the stencil blocked from the light are washed away with water, thus creating a negative stencil, from which a positive image may be printed.

Direct/indirect stencils consist of a light-sensitive emulsion precoated on a plastic support backing (Cappilex is the most common), which is adhered to the mesh and dried before exposure. Developed for fine detail printing, they come in a variety of thickness coatings. Due to their expense, they tend not to be used much for fine-art printing. They have less exposure latitude than most direct emulsions. This means they are less forgiving to stencils that are too dense or too pale, which can normally be compensated for by increasing or decreasing the exposure length. The marks that an artist makes are, by their perverse nature, nearly always too pale or too dense by commercial reproduction standards.

Indirect stencils are a light-sensitive emulsion precoated on a plastic support backing, which is exposed and washed out before being adhered to the screen. They are very expensive to use and so tend to be avoided for this reason. They are also primarily made for solvent-based printing.

Stencils are perhaps the major factor of change within the adoption of water-based screenprint systems. Direct working on the screen was one of the advantages of solvent-based screenprint. It was very easy to paint a water-soluble filler directly onto the screen, then print with a solvent-based ink. Now this is no longer so easy. By eliminating solvents, it is no longer possible to paint directly onto the screen. On the other hand, editioning studios who have always had the necessity to remake a screen if the current one broke down, long ago gave up the facility of making the stencil directly on the screen, and have transferred the autographic qualities to hand-drawn stencil films.

The change to direct emulsion finally permeated all sectors of the fine-art screenprinting arena. A few enlightened individuals and institutions such as the Royal College of Art, have used these products for many years, but for most of us, the change from indirect films such as Five Star and Novastar was slow and painful.

This reluctance was not surprising, given the need for purpose-built printing down frames, drying cupboards that are lightfast and preferably a quartz halide light source. The long-term benefits for art schools and workshops are the markedly lower costs of these products and the safer chemicals used in the processing. Which brand of direct emulsion to use is a matter of personal preference. I use mainly Folex Dc200, only because I keep stencils on screens for long periods and find this emulsion will de-coat easily under such circumstances. The emulsions come in three different forms.

'Ten Burantinos' by Igor Makarevich, Russia. Screenprint on Arches 88 paper, 56 x 71cm, ed. 46, 1998.
Printed by Dennis O Neil at Hand Print Workshop International, Alexandria, Virginia, USA. Photo courtesy of Hand Print Workshop.

Dichromates (e.g. Seriset).
These are the original direct emulsions. They are cheap to use but have distinct health and safety disadvantages. The dichromate used in their manufacture is not very biodegradable, and you need the use of bleach or other strong alkaline solutions to de-coat them from the screen. They have a very short shelf-life when mixed. They are still used by some textile printers as they are cheap to buy. This is compensated for by the expense of removing them. They are not very sensitive and will not pick up fine detail. I do not regard these emulsions as suitable for general studio use.

Diazo-based (e.g. Folex Dc200, Kiwicol Poly plus W)
These come in two parts: the emulsion and a sensitiser. They have a very wide exposure latitude, and will cope well with being under- or over-exposed, without breaking down or filling in. They are therefore very good at dealing with badly made artwork. The dual cure versions can be used for both solvent and water-based inks. Their only problem is their lack of a long-term shelf life. Once mixed under normal conditions, with the lid kept firmly in place they will last for approximately 6 to 8 weeks; if kept in a refrigerator they will last approximately 3 to 4 months. These products are de-coated with chemicals that are less harmful, much easier to use, and do not cause the same health and environmental problems. I recommend these as the best option for most users.

One-pot emulsions, sometimes known as SBQ (e.g. Folex Dc500).
These are the latest generation of emulsions that in performance terms for most printmaking, show little difference from the diazo-based products. Their advantage lies in an extended shelf life: they will keep for long periods without showing signs of thickening. They are de-coated with the same chemicals as the diazo-based products. The minus side is they prefer correct exposure periods, so any under- or over-exposure can result in a stencil that remains tacky, causing newspaper to stick to them whilst blotting. They are good if you use emulsion only very occasionally, other-wise I recommend you use diazo-based emulsion (also known as dual cure).

Coating troughs

Direct emulsions are transferred to the screen using a coating trough. This is a shallow U-shaped trough sealed at the ends, deep enough to hold 2 or 3 cm of emulsion. It has a lip on the front edge which is pressed firmly against the back of the screen when coating (by the back I mean the side of the mesh away from the frame). When drawn steadily up the surface of the mesh from the base, the trough will leave a thin, even deposit of emulsion (see opposite).

Coating trough. Do not skimp – fill the trough with a generous layer of emulsion and return the excess to the pot after use.

Coating the screen. Use one long steady pull with a coating trough slightly narrower than the screen and make sure there are no bubbles in the emulsion.

These are the golden rules to using emulsions:

Ensure the coating trough is spotlessly clean with no nicks or notches, especially the blade (the back edge of the blade particularly), with no traces of residue or dried emulsion.

Keep the lid tightly on the pot of emulsion and ideally keep it in a 'fridge' to make sure there are no hard lumps or thickening of the emulsion.

Make sure the screens are properly and tightly stretched before coating to ensure you use the minimum amount of emulsion. One coat with spotting out to fill in any small holes in the stencil caused by dust or other particles on the glass is adequate for most circumstances.

Coating (illustration of method)

Coating does not need to be undertaken under safe light conditions as long as the screens are not exposed to bright direct sunlight, the emulsion is used and replaced quickly into the pot, and the screen is not left to dry in daylight. Once they are coated, they need to be kept in the dark or under safe light conditions. Screens will last several days once coated; after this they need to be reclaimed by cleaning off the emulsion and then re-coated to guarantee good stencils. Direct sunlight will affect the emulsion if it is exposed to light for more than 5 minutes.

Fill the coating trough with a generous layer of emulsion, 2 or 3cm (1in.) it is easier to scrape the excess back into the pot rather than run out. Prop the screen at an approximately 60° angle with the top furthest away from you. Hold the trough against the screen at the bottom and tip until there is a continuous line of emulsion across the trough resting against the screen. Then coat the back of the screen with a single pull starting at the bottom and working to the top.

All the manufacturers of emulsion will tell you to coat several times on both sides of the screen. The purpose of multiple coating is to give good stencil strength and a totally consistent result from one exposure to the next. Neither attribute is of particular interest to the fine-art printer. The primary concern of multiple coating is to create a strong stencil which will last for many thousands of prints, something not usually required by artists. In fact, we have found that not only does a single coat save money, but it is possible to draw out much finer detail on a short exposure, from a delicate stencil (which would be deemed unusable by industry) than you can with a multiple coat.

Drying

Most importantly, always force-dry screens with heat. In California, at a well-known editioning studio I visited, the outside temperature is always hot. After coating they prop screens against a wall in the darkroom to dry naturally, but due to the relative humidity as the screens dry they trap a layer of moisture droplets inside the emulsion. When the screens are exposed, the moisture droplets scatter the light making very poor stencils. It shocked me to find that this lack of force-drying, combined with the absence of an integrator (a light source controlled by a photo-electric cell to read light density), meant that they could not produce high-definition stencils. Do not use too great a heat; the ideal temperature is in the region of 35° to 40°C.

However, it is possible to prop the screens to dry in a darkroom with a fan heater blowing warm air constantly over them until dry. The best solution is a drying cabinet (see Chapter Seven on Studio set-up)

Making the stencil

Once the screen has been coated and is thoroughly dry, the screen is ready for the artwork and exposure. First, clean the glass of the exposure unit (see Chapter Seven) and make sure it has no scratches in the area you are going to place the artwork upon. Place the film positive or artwork to be exposed the correct way round on the glass, with the drawn or emulsion side upwards, this is so that any text would read the correct way round when you place the positive on the glass. Then place the screen on top, with the back of the screen in contact with the artwork, the frame of the screen facing upwards. Make sure there is at least a 13cm (5in.) border between the image and the inside edge of the screen frame (see page 41, Screens).

At this point, lower the lid of the vacuum top, and turn on the vacuum. Or, if using a very simple exposure unit (see Chapter Seven, Studio set-up), place a rubber sheet, a board and a weight on the screen. The purpose of the vacuum or weight is to ensure that the artwork has the tightest possible contact with the screen, so that when it is exposed, the minimum amount of light possible can creep around the edges of the stencil. This is particularly important for the fine detail of halftones. If light creeps round the edges, much of the detail can be lost. It is also important that the artwork is right-reading and emulsion side up. This means that the information on the film backing (support) is on the uppermost surface. If a halftone is exposed with the information on the underside, the thickness of the film support layer can allow the light to creep around the dots, thus filling in the finest tones.

Exposure times

Exposure times will vary depending on the light source, the age of the bulbs, the power of the bulbs and the distance of the artwork from the bulbs. It is therefore not possible to give any indication on times. The only way to ascertain timing for a particular set up is to do a test strip, as in darkroom photography. Tape a black mask to the glass between the light source and the screen and make a series of multiple exposures.

Do this by setting your light source at the manufacturer's recommended time and then make three exposures, one standard, one 10% shorter and one 10% longer. Then develop the screen and choose the timing that gives the most detail but will not break down easily when printing. If you have no idea at all of the length of exposure required, mask one fifth of the stencil with black paper and set the exposure at a given

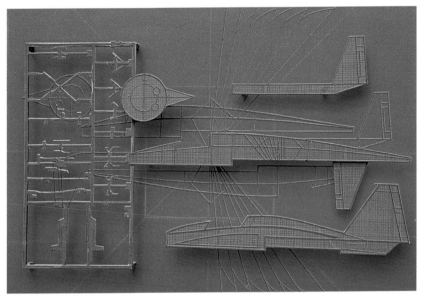

'Red Alert' by Penny Brewill, UK. Screenprint construction. 32 x 46cm, 1999.

time, say 10 units, turn on the light source, expose the screen, then mask a further fifth of the screen and expose for another 10 units and so on until you have five exposures. Develop the screen. If it shows little signs of exposure, you will not be able to see any signs of an image in the mesh and, in other words, most of the stencil washes away. Repeat the test with increased exposure times, say 50 units. If it is over-exposed and nothing washes away, repeat the test with decreased exposure times.

However, a few general points may come in useful. Diazo emulsions have an extremely good range of latitude, once an average exposure time has been established. It can be adjusted to suit differing artwork. Greater lengths of time are usually required for films of the True Grain type than for bureau-produced film positives. This is because these textured films are translucent, and therefore slightly less light will pass through them. The same applies for the laser films (Folex). Delicate washes need less time than black solids. Also, remember this is a photographic process. Therefore similar adjustments and results to stencil exposure can be made to those used for normal darkroom photography. In other words, a thin piece of artwork can be compensated for with less exposure. Likewise, a very dense piece of artwork can be compensated for with a longer exposure.

Ultra-violet (UV) light sources

UV light sources usually come in two forms. The first is UV bulbs or tubes, in the simplest of exposure units a single bulb with a starter and ballast, to multiple bulbs or rows of tubes. This form of light source is normally housed in some form of box or cabinet, with doors that open to expose the screen to the light source. An example is the exposure units made by the Graphoscreen Company.

The other common form is quartz halide. These usually come as a free-standing light (the light source) with a shutter mechanism installed in the light unit and a separate exposure frame (a printing down frame). This contains the glass sheet and a vacuum top to maintain good contact between the screen and the glass. The screen and stencil are normally put into place with the glass in a horizontal position. Then once the vacuum is turned on the whole frame is swung through 90° to face the light source. This type of light source is brighter than the standard UV bulbs and quartz halide light sources range from a half to 5kW.

Light sources. This is a 1kW quartz halide light source, with a printing down frame in the background.

All UV light sources need time to warm up when turned on and time to cool down after use. Attempting to turn them on straight after they have been turned off can damage the bulbs. 1kW quartz halide is generally best.

Washing out

Once the screen has been exposed, it should be washed out swiftly. Do not expose the screen in daylight as the unexposed areas (those that have been blocked by the artwork) will begin to expose. All of the new generation of direct stencils are washed with cold water. The easiest way is to use normal tap pressure and a spray head. Gently wash the back of the screen first to make sure it is wet, then turn the screen around and wash away the unexposed parts of the stencil. It is very important to wash the whole area of screen coating, not just the parts that have the image area. If the screen is not washed thoroughly all the unexposed coating will not wash away. This residue can block the screens and cause problems whilst printing. Added to this the stencil coating is mildly acidic. If the residue is not removed, this can cross-link with some of the acrylic inks and cause them to harden and dry in on the screen. This is why some inks require a mild alkaline coating to be washed over the screen before printing (see Chapter Six, Inks), in order to neutralise the acidity of the screen emulsions. When the stencil is properly washed, return it to the drying cabinet.

It is possible for the small-scale user to wash screens out in a large sink or the bath. Care must be taken to ensure that the screen has been thoroughly washed out. The residue washed away can build up and cause blocked drains in a domestic environment.

Screen fillers

Screen fillers are primarily used to block out the small holes in the stencil. These are usually caused by dust on the glass of the exposure frame. The screen fillers are also used to block out parts of the stencil no longer needed after one printing has finished and they are too close to the next printing to be avoided. Also, some basic alterations to the stencil can be made with filler if necessary. In the past, fillers were used by artists to paint stencils directly onto the screen.

The most common complaint with water-based screenprinting is the lack of a number of good screen fillers for hand-painting stencils. I only know of one good filler. There is a very good commercial reason for this. As previously stated, screenprinting products are primarily developed for industry and are adapted and adopted by artists. The costs of developing and stocking a screen filler has to make commercial sense. Industry does not have a need for a removable filler, and the art market buys so little of these products (perhaps one 5 litre/9 pint container per year) that no company is going to spend a lot of time developing such a filler. Having said that, a very good product is made by Gibbon Marler in the UK. It is called Safeguard Water Soluble Green Filler, and if mixed 50/50 with water, makes an excellent removable product with the right combination of de-coating products (which are Kissel and Wolf A9 extra and Pregasol F).

Spotting and taping

Once the screen has dried after being washed, the stencil can be spotted out. Use the water-based filler as described above and a small fine paint-brush. This is nearly always necessary if only one coat of direct emulsion is used as described above. Do not be over-generous with the filler; if too thick a layer is put on, it can be hard to remove from the screen during cleaning.

The screen needs to be taped around the edges where the screen emulsion has not reached. The problem lies in finding a suitable tape that does not leave a sticky residue behind after use – trial and error with different brands is the best recommendation I can make. I use a parcel tape made by Sellotape that has a blue-printed inner core with the name Sellotape continuously printed upon it.

Spotting and filling is used to remove the pinholes in the stencil caused by dust and light bouncing off the edge of the film positive.

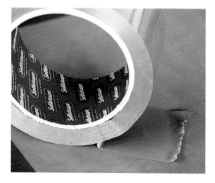

Parcel tape (note this brand is the only one we have found that does not leave a sticky residue on the screen).

Direct stencil removal, cleaning the screen

Whilst most of the chemicals now used for cleaning screens no longer carry hazard warning signs, it is still recommended for good health and safety practice to wear safety goggles, rubber gloves and a protective apron. Ear protectors should always be worn when using a high-pressure washer.

Once the screen has been printed, clean off the excess ink. Place the screen in a washing trough (see Chapter Seven) and wash away the remaining ink with water. With the screen still wet, a small amount of

Washing out with ear protectors; water hitting off the tight screen can cause a loud drumming sound.

de-coating chemical is applied to both sides of the screen with a brush. This should be left for a couple of minutes in order for the chemical to soften the emulsion, before blasting the screen with the high-pressure washer. The chemical and excess emulsion should be gently washed off with just normal tap pressure and a hose to avoid spraying chemicals around the room. Then the screen is blasted from both sides with the pressure washer. This is normally sufficient to remove all of the stencil and any residue of ink remaining in the screen. If there is any stencil left blocking the screen, repeat the above procedure.

Any dried ink which will not be removed by the pressure washer will require one of three remedies, listed in order of increasing health hazard. First, try washing the affected part of the screen with a mild alkaline such as *Mr Muscle* kitchen cleaner. If this is unsuccessful, then secondly try using a water-soluble safe screen wash such as Marler Safeguard; or thirdly use an alkaline cleaning paste such as Pregan. These products should be handled with care. Carefully read instructions before use. There is another remedy which is the most drastic and is used only for extremely clogged screens where the only alternative may be to scrap the screen. This is to pour very hot water, almost boiling, onto the screen, which should soften the acrylic enough for it to be blasted from the screen. If the water is too hot you may dissolve the polyester mesh. The line between the water being hot enough to soften the ink and being too hot and dissolving the mesh is very fine. Good housekeeping, by this I mean cleaning screens thoroughly and quickly after printing, should avoid this scenario.

Removing ghosting (staining)

If the ghosting is very bad and affecting the performance of the screen, or if it is becoming impossible to see through for registration, the only alternative is to clean the screen with an alkaline cleaning paste such as Pregan. Brush this sparingly onto both sides of a damp screen, leave for 20 minutes, and then hose off gently with tap water, making sure all the paste is removed before blasting with the pressure washer.

Note: these pastes are extremely caustic and must be handled with great care. Goggles, gloves and a protective apron must be worn.

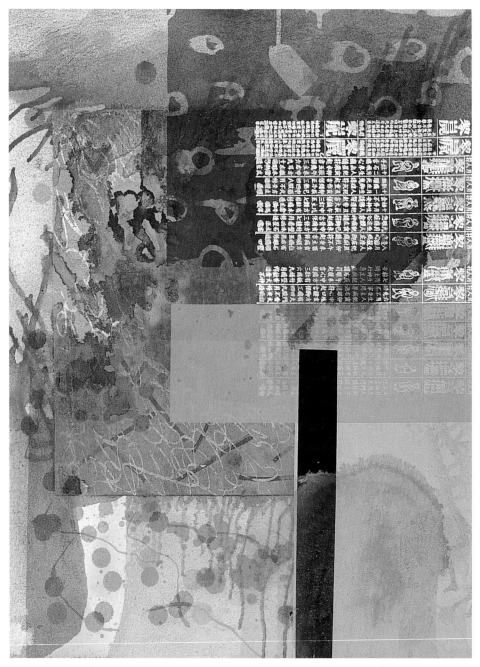

'Untitled' by Dale Deveraux Barker, UK. Screenprint monoprint (oil based), 55 x 38cm, 1999. Printed by the artist.
Photo permission the artist.

Chapter 4
INKS

This chapter will deal with the different types of ink available, which inks are recommended for specific tasks, ink mixing, storage, effects obtainable, and printing resists for etching plates.

Over the last five years an ever-increasing number of new water-based inks have entered the market. To clarify some misconceptions, each of the inks carries some hydrocarbon-based solvent (normally less than 2%). Most of these solvents are of the ester type used in things such as lipstick manufacture. Hydrocarbon solvents are replaced by water in mixing and cleaning. To my knowledge there are now 28 different water-based inks available. They can be categorised into four main types and I publish here the results of part of a research project undertaken at the University of the West of England into the first 12 inks on the market. Of the 16 new inks on the market, none to my knowledge are significantly different from one of the four categories listed.

Ink types

The four main types of water-based ink:

1. Acrylic paint for artists: these are mixed with a screenprinting medium to make them suitable for printing;

2. Industrial inks developed for the screenprinting paper and board industry are produced by the traditional solvent ink manufacturers, and are mostly in their infancy, having not yet received a great deal of interest by potential developers;

3. Pre-mixed inks specifically developed for screenprinting use by small-scale manufacturers with the specialist user in mind;

4. Textile inks mixed with a binder: these inks have existed for many years but are not normally considered for printmaking for two reasons. First, dye is used rather than pigment, which makes the colour very fugitive; secondly, as these inks are intended for use on cloth, there has been little incentive to reduce the water content resulting in a marked tendency to buckle paper.

INKS

Inks tested

ACRYLIC PAINTS

Manufacturer	Trade Name
Chroma Acrylics	Chromacryl
Lascaux	Gouache
	Studio
Daler Rowney	System 3

INDUSTRIAL INKS

Manufacturer	Trade Name
Small Products	Aquagraphic
Ash Coatings	Aqualex
Coates Lorrilux	Hydroprint
Marler	Paintbox
JT Keep	Sinvaqua 'SQE'
TW Graphics	1000 Series

PRE-MIXED ARTISTS' INKS

Manufacturer	Trade Name
Hunt	Speedball

INKS AVAILABLE AND NOT TESTED

Createx, Golden, Marabu, Quimovil, Proll, Screen Colour Systems, Sun Chemical, Visprox, VFP, TW Graphics 5000 Series, Union, Sericol

Test methodology

Five colours from each range of ink were tested with 28 different criteria in mind. These criteria covered four broad areas: colour quality, ink quality, base quality (where applicable), and general observations. In order to assess these qualities, the inks were printed on a 5 x 5 grid on a black line cross. Samples were printed on a standard heavy-duty 200gsm cartridge paper. Somerset white 300gsm hot press and on a cheap 140gsm recycled cartridge so that quality could be assessed on a variety of paper surfaces. A Svecia semi-automatic screenprint machine was used with 120t screens stretched to 14 Newtons per cm^2 to standardise speed and blade pressure, etc. The inks were printed and analysed by a group of experienced printmakers including technicians, artists and edition printers to give a broad range of experience in using screenprinting inks and in order to reduce personal preferences and habits as much as possible. Whilst it is hoped that the results and conclusions are as objective as possible, it is recognised there is bound to be a subjective element in the evaluations. This is intended to give a guide to the relative pros and cons to the various inks available so that the printmaker may select the appropriate ink for each job. Each of the five colours of every ink tested was given points out

	1000 series	Aquagraphic	Aqualex	Chromacryl	Gouache	Hydroprint	Paintbox	Sinvaqua 'SQE'	Speedball	Studio (Acrylic)	System 3
Colour quality											
Transparency Average	6.5	5.3	6.0	6.5	7.5	7.8	7.5	5.8	7.3	7.0	**8.0**
Colour strength	8.4	6.6	7.4	5.0	6.2	7.9	**8.4**	7.4	6.5	6.4	6.9
Chalkiness	7.9	5.5	7.6	5.0	6.2	7.0	**8.2**	7.0	6.8	7.2	7.5
Colour-mixing quality	**9.0**	5.5	6.3	6.0	7.0	7.0	8.4	6.8	8.0	7.0	7.9
Colour-overlay quality	7.8	5.3	6.8	5.3	7.6	6.0	**8.9**	6.5	7.0	6.5	6.5
Colour intensity	**9.8**	5.4	7.6	4.4	6.4	8.5	9.0	6.0	7.0	7.8	7.2
Balance through range	**8.3**	6.0	**8.3**	6.7	**8.3**	7.7	6.0	7.3	7.0	**8.3**	8.0
Subjective quality	**8.8**	6.2	5.8	5.3	6.0	5.0	7.8	4.8	7.4	6.8	8.0
Ink quality											
Texture	**9.0**	7.4	7.6	6.6	7.0	7.5	7.6	6.0	7.6	7.6	8.0
Mixing quality	**10.**	n/a	6.0	5.6	7.0	n/a	7.0	7.0	9.0	7.0	6.8
Surface finish	8.0	6.6	**9.6**	4.0	5.2	6.8	7.0	8.8	6.2	6.4	6.0
Base quality											
Viscosity	**8.0**	n/a	n/a	n/a	7.0	n/a	n/a	n/a	n/a	7.0	7.6
Smoothness	**8.0**	n/a	n/a	n/a	6.0	n/a	n/a	n/a	n/a	6.0	7.0
Coverage	**9.0**	n/a	n/a	n/a	8.0	n/a	n/a	n/a	n/a	8.0	8.0
Printing quality											
Fine line details	8.0	8.0	6.0	7.2	6.0	**9.0**	7.0	8.0	7.0	7.0	8.0
Creep	8.8	8.8	8.0	8.2	9.0	10.	8.0	8.0	7.8	**9.0**	**9.0**
Thickening on screen	6.6	8.8	7.4	**9.0**	**9.0**	3.0	8.0	8.0	**9.0**	**9.0**	**9.0**
Cockling of paper	7.6	4.0	5.8	7.0	4.8	6.8	7.0	4.0	**8.2**	5.2	6.0
Ease of washing up	5.2	7.8	2.0	**10.**	**10.**	3.2	6.8	1.4	8.0	8.4	8.8
Screen staining	6.4	8.4	4.0	**10.**	**10.**	4.0	7.2	6.0	7.8	9.8	8.2
Coverage	**9.0**	5.6	7.0	5.6	8.0	8.2	8.0	7.0	7.8	7.2	7.0
Drying in	7.0	**9.0**	4.2	**9.0**	7.0	3.0	7.8	5.4	8.0	6.6	8.5
Quality of solid	**9.6**	6.4	8.8	4.0	5.8	6.8	7.2	7.8	6.4	7.0	6.8
Self solvency	6.0	6.0	4.0	**9.0**	6.0	3.0	7.0	5.0	7.0	6.0	8.0
General observations											
Odour	5.0	8.0	2.0	6.8	10.	2.2	6.0	1.0	8.8	9.0	**10**
Drying times	9.5	**10.**	9.9	8.0	2.2	7.6	**10.**	9.9	**10.**	3.5	9.5
Irritant properties	7.0	8.0	2.0	8.4	10.	2.0	6.6	1.0	8.0	10.	**10.**
Cost	7.5	8.6	7.2	9.5	7.0	6.3	3.5	5.7	1.0	7.0	**10.**
AVERAGE SCORE	**7.9**	7.0	6.3	6.9	7.2	6.1	7.4	6.1	7.4	7.3	**7.9**

of 10. Only the average mark is listed here. In the cost category, the approximate price of a litre of ready-to-use ink was calculated and given a value.

Conclusions

Broadly speaking, the acrylic group of paints with a screenprinting base dry very slowly in the screen, so they are the perfect inks for fine-detail printing (e.g., Daler-Rowney, Lascaux). They are also consequently a very forgiving ink for students too, but the colour quality is not very luminescent and can appear slightly murky as overlays. These inks can be far and away the cheapest (Daler Rowney and Chroma Acrylics Chromacryl). They have a tendency to buckle paper so cannot be used for lightweight substrates.

The industrial inks are more varied. Some have a better luminosity (TW Graphics 1000 Series) and scuff resistance (Marler Paintbox and Coates Lorrilux Hydroprint); and in others the printed appearance resembles the quality of solvent-based inks (Ash Coatings Aqualex). They often print well on other substrates (Small Products Aquagraphic and JT Keep Sinvaqua 'SQE') (see substrate chart), but tend to have limited colour ranges. The exception is the TW Graphics 1000 range which scores one of the highest colour-range marks of all the inks. They also tend to dry into the screen very quickly and so can be very difficult to wash out.

Colour quality varies hugely across the range of inks and does not generally bear any relation to ease of printing. Colour quality is one of the most subjective areas, along with the overall quality of an individual ink range, and it is over these particular tests that there was most dispute between the individual tester's judgements; for these criteria varied according to the tester's background. All these criteria have been combined to present an aggregate in the published test results.

The quality of the inks themselves reflects the manufacturers' intended use. The acrylic paints tend to be very thick and thrixotropic (giving them a thick consistency similar to hair gel). To traditional users of solvent-based ink, these present a major shift in printmaking practice. The quality of the industrial inks is very similar to the traditional solvent inks, but these inks often require an alkaline solution washed over the screen to reduce the acidity of the photostencil.

The drying-in times on the screen vary enormously, from Daler Rowney System 3 which takes a long time to dry, to Coates Lorrilux Hydroprint which dries rapidly in the screen. The acrylic inks, e.g., Lascaux Gouache and Studio, Chroma Acrylics Chromacryl and Daler Rowney are very easy to wash up, again making them a useful learning tool for students. Some of the industrial inks can be more complicated (TW Graphics 1000 Series and Marler Paintbox), but for the more sophisticated printmaker these difficulties are offset by the added colour and variety of surface qualities. Cockling (buckling) is a problem for nearly all the inks but the two inks with the best scores are Hunt Speedball and TW Graphics 1000 Series. Otherwise it is recommended that one use heavier stock than would be normal practice (at least 250gsm paper).

As regards smell and irritant properties, in our tests Lascaux Gouache and Studio and Daler Rowney System 3 came out best subjectively, but it must be noted that Hunt Speedball conforms to US health and safety standards of non-toxicity. The cost scores should be taken only as an approximate, as the prices are based only on the five colours tested. In some ranges colours such as magenta can be four or five times the price of a standard colour. The chart shows that cost is not necessarily indicative of quality.

Inks for particular purposes

Having used these inks for over seven years, I now use a particular brand of ink for a particular job or mix several brands together to create the desired effect or consistency. This was always the case with solvent-based inks. The following are some useful guidelines and methods I have found effective. Consequently, much of the decision-making process is non-subjective and based on personal preferences.

Studio and high-quality work

I use the TW graphics 1000 Series because of its colour intensity, versatility of bases, and its visual and aesthetic qualities, combined with its ability not to cockle paper. These factors outweigh its disadvantages, namely it dries on the screen fairly quickly and is not the easiest ink to wash up. This is the ink recommended for studio and high-quality work. The Marler Paintbox and Hunt Speedball both performed well and are some people's preferred option. The disadvantage of Paintbox is its lack of a red-biased blue, making mixing some ranges of colour extremely difficult. The Hunt Speedball is expensive to buy and use in the UK. Union ink, though not tested, comes well recommended from users in the US.

Student and communal studio work

The Daler-Rowney scores best for this purpose in the UK due to its cost. It is a very good general-purpose ink with slow drying times. This price advantage is not so good in Europe or the US. In this case inks such as the Lascaux or Golden have very similar properties and score well on colour quality and ease of use.

Metallic ink effects

The biggest difference for mixing metallic lies in the viscosity of the solvent used to create the ink. In solvent inks you have a more viscous solution. So metallic particles will remain in suspension throughout the

'*Mummer*' by Allan Mann, Australia. Multiple glass screenprinted with applied gold leaf and silverleaf with sandblasting, 26 x 18 x 5.5cms, 1994.
Photo permission the artist.

ink more readily. With a water-based ink, the particles will fall through the water content very quickly. A pre-mixed metallic ink is consequently not very effective. Therefore, to make an effective printing ink, the following guidelines need to be followed.

First take a very small quantity of medium or base, add the finest metallic powder you can obtain and stir in slowly until you have created a thick paste. Make sure all the powder is thoroughly mixed in. Now add further medium stirring constantly until the ink is the desired consistency for printing. Print with the ink straight away. The ink will be suitable for printing for a few hours at the most, then the metallic particles will sink to the bottom. When this occurs the ink will no longer produce a good metallic finish on the paper. At this point dispense with the remaining ink and mix a fresh batch. Once the metallic powder has settled out, it cannot be redistributed throughout the printing medium.

Printing gloss

The most effective water-based gloss I have found is made by TW inks – they make a gloss medium and a gloss over-print; both give a good finish. If you need to print a gloss and you are using one of the acrylic paint systems (Daler-Rowney, Lascaux), you should add acrylic gloss mediums to the ink. Be careful that the combined proportion of gloss medium and colour does not exceed the 50% total colour to medium ratio recommended for these systems. In this instance, gloss medium counts as colour.

Printing etching plates

Screenprinting can be an effective method of creating a photographic image onto an etching plate, if the traditional methods of creating photo etching are not available. Two methods of printing a photographic image with water-based ink directly onto an etching plate may be used. In order to print an image, the plate has to be first de-greased and dried in the normal manner with whiting and ammonia (see Walter Chamberlain, *Etching*, Thames & Hudson).

Firstly, using a water-proof medium, such as TW, it is possible to print a negative image on the plate, by coating the plate in aquatint dust in the normal manner, and then biting the plate in acid or for safety reasons, ferric chloride, if using copper. The waterproof ink will resist the acid sufficiently to create a full photographic image on the plate. The resulting

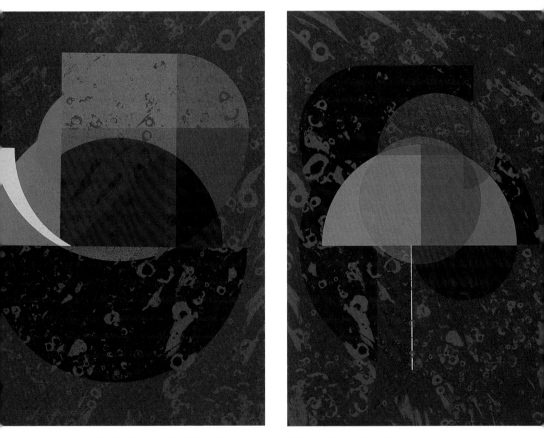

Above left: *'Golden Section 9'* by Steve Hoskins. Oil-based ink, 76 x 56cm.
Above right: *'Golden Section 10'* by Steve Hoskins. Water-based ink, 76 x 56cm.
These two prints were made and exhibited to prove that, technically, people could not discern a visible difference between oil and water-based inks.

INKS

plate can then be cleaned with methylated spirit to remove the aquatint and a mild alkaline to remove the screenprinted resist.

Secondly, if using an acrylic-based system (Daler Rowney, etc.), it is possible to print a positive image on the plate. This ink is then treated in the manner known as sugar lift in etching. To assist in seeing what is happening on the plate, it is better to use printing medium with some colour added. The addition of up to 20% icing sugar dissolved into the ink assists the speed of the process.

Once the image has been printed onto the de-greased plate and the ink is dry, the plate is then coated with a thin solution of etching stopping out varnish thinned down with white spirit. This is left to dry preferably overnight. Next prepare a bath of hot water larger than the size of the plate, lower the plate into the bath until it is completely submerged. Gently brush the surface of the plate with a feather or very soft paintbrush. The printed parts should expand and lift away the covering coat of varnish. More hot water may need to be added to the bath to assist this process. When all the varnish has lifted off the plate, remove from the bath, dry, then aquatint and treat as a normal etching plate.

'*Still 1*' by Kristian Krokfors, Finland. 66.7 x 54.5cm, ed. 20, 1999 (published 2000). Printed and published by Pratt Contemporary Art, Kent, UK.

Chapter 5
PAPER

This chapter covers how paper is made, sizes, weight and surface quality,
which paper to use for screenprinting and handling paper.

■ All paper is made from cellulose fibre. In Europe until the 19th century, paper was traditionally made from rags. Artists' paper, in the main, uses cotton linters, rather than rags, as its primary source. Other plant fibres such as Esparto, Kozu, Eucalyptus and Mulberry are also used. Commercial papers for printing tend to use cellulose derived from wood or wood pulp. The cellulose fibres are broken down by beating and mixed with water to form a pulp. The mixture is very dilute. The relationship of pulp to water will have a direct effect on the weight of a sheet of paper. The sheet of paper is then manufactured from the pulp by one of three methods: handmade, mould-made (made on a cylinder mould machine) or machine-made (made on a Fourdrinier machine). How a sheet of paper is made often has more effect on the printing qualities than its weight, sizing or surface. All these factors need to be taken into account when choosing a suitable sheet to print upon.

Handmade paper begins with the paper pulp in a large vat, within which the pulp is agitated to evenly disperse the fibres throughout the water. A *mould* (which consists of two parts: firstly a rigid wooden frame stretched with a fine wire mesh and a surrounding frame called a deckle to contain the pulp as it is lifted from the vat) is dipped into the vat and lifted out with a gentle shaking action to evenly distribute the fibres across the surface of the mould. The water drains from the mould and during this process a small proportion of pulp seeps under the deckle frame thus creating the characteristic deckle edge of handmade paper. The sheet of wet pulp is then transferred to a felt blanket (*couched*), a further blanket is placed on top and another sheet is made and a further blanket is placed on top. When a sufficient number of sheets have been made, the pile (called a *stand*) is placed into a press to squeeze out the excess moisture. The sheets are then separated from the felts, the felts are returned for re-use and the sheets are laid upon one another to form a *pack* about 10cm (4in.) thick. Unless a rough finish is required, the pack is placed between zinc plates and pressed again. The first pressing leaves marks from the threads in the felts on the sheets; the second reduces these irregularities, producing a smoother sheet. The sheets are then parted and dried. This method of

PAPER

manufacture means the orientation of the fibres has no particular direction as is the case with the other methods. This makes for an inherently strong stable sheet of paper.

Commercial handmade sheets used by printmakers would include papers such as J. Barcham Green, Twinrocker, Richard De Bas or Two Rivers.

Mould-made paper starts with the pulp in a vat as in hand-made paper, though in this case the vat contains a rotating cylinder covered in a fine steel mesh which is partially immersed in the watery pulp. The paper then moulds itself to the outside of the cylinder as it rotates through the water. When the cylinder reaches the top of its revolution, the paper is couched off onto a felt, then onto a series of rollers to be further processed. At this point the roll of paper may be sized and/or given a different surface finish. It is only after the end of the manufacturing process that the paper is torn down to size. Because of the nature of the machine, which is usually run very slowly, there is a difference in properties and grain direction between the long and short directions of the paper, but not so pronounced as for commercially manufactured machine-made paper. Commercial mould-mades include Somerset, Arches, Zerkall and Fabriano.

Machine-made paper is made by starting with a pulp in low concentration in water, this is often of a lower quality than is the case in either mould or hand-made paper. The pulp is stored in a large tank (the breast box) above

Above: the cylinder on a mould-mesh machine. The big mesh cylinder in the vat is known as a dandy roll.

Right: Paper coming out of the vat onto the dandy roll.

a horizontal fast-moving wire mesh belt. The sheet of paper is formed by flowing a steady stream of pulp onto the belt, excess water is drained away through the wire mesh and is assisted by a vacuum pump. At the end of the wire belt the paper is couched off and, as in mould-made paper, will undergo further processing – finally to be wound onto large reels. The paper is then cut to sheet size elsewhere. This type of machine is known as a Fourdrinier machine after the Fourdrinier

Fourdrinier machine. The paper pulp is sprayed onto the belt just below the breast box.

brothers who invented the machine in 1803. Nearly all paper made commercially is made by this method. Drawing Cartridges and all commercial print papers are the most common to be used by printmakers.

Common paper sizes

Paper size	Dimensions in inches	Dimensions in cm
Royal	20 x 25in.	51 x 64cm
Imperial	22 x 30in.	56 x 76cm
Double Elephant	27 x 40in.	68.8 x 101.6cm
A0	33.11 x 46.81in.	84 x 119cm
A1	23.39 x 33.11in.	59.5 x 84cm
A2	23.39 x 16.54in.	42 x 59.5cm
A3	16.54 x 11.69in.	29.7 x 42cm
A4	8.27 x 11.69in.	21 x 29.7cm
A5	5.83 x 8.27in.	14.8 x 21cm
A6	4.13 x 5.83in.	10.5 x 14.8cm

Weight of paper

Weight of paper or thickness is measured in one of two main ways. The most common and in general use since metrication in the paper trade is grams per square metre (abbreviated to gsm or g/m^2) and literally refers to the weight of one square metre of any given sheet of paper.

This replaces the old system of measuring paper weight, taken as the weight of 500 sheets (referred to as a ream) in whatever size the paper happened to be. Therefore a 140lb Imperial would weigh 300g, but a 140lb royal would be 600g and twice as thick and heavy as the Imperial sheet. A brief attempt to define some of the poundage weights to common size and grams is listed in the table above.

PAPER

Paper size	Weight in gsm	Weight in lbs	
Imperial 56 x 76cm	150gsm	Imperial	72lb
Imperial 56 x 76cm	180gsm	Imperial	90lb
Imperial 56 x 76cm	300gsm	Imperial	140lb
Imperial 56 x 76cm	410gsm	Imperial	200lb

Surface of the paper

The three most common surfaces for artists are ROUGH, NOT and HP (hot-pressed). In the main these apply to handmade and mould-made papers. The terms were first introduced in the early 19th century, when HP stood for a hot-pressed or glazed surface, this meant after pressing the sheet would either be further pressed several times to produce a smooth surface or would be passed between hot or glazing rollers. NOT meant quite literally not hot-pressed and referred to the surface of the paper as it was made with no further treatments, ROUGH was generally induced by using a courser blanket, then only pressing the paper once. The definitions now are taken to mean:

HP	a perfectly smooth surface
NOT	natural surface with a slight grain
ROUGH	course surface with a large and open grain

A watermark is just a slightly thinner section of paper. It is created by sewing or welding wire thread to the mould or Dandy roll. The difference between *wove* and *laid* paper is due to the type of mould used. Laid paper is the earliest type of mould and consists of wire laid in lines around which were wired or woven chain wires. This type of paper has a very characteristic surface which most people recognise in Ingres drawing papers. This surface is also recognised in many Japanese handmade papers, due to the type of bamboo mould used. Wove paper was introduced in 1757 and the mould was made of woven wire. This is the mould used today for the majority of paper.

Sizing

Paper with no size or surface coating added is called waterleaf. Inks will bleed into the surface in the same manner as blotting paper, which is a waterleaf type sheet. Sizing is therefore an operation during paper manufacture which gives the paper a water resistance to a greater or lesser degree. It is achieved by the addition of chemical additives. Typical products used are the traditional gelatine and rosin and the more recent Aquapel. As the degree of sizing affects its absorption of water, the degree of sizing is an important factor in the choice of paper for water-based screenprinting.

A consideration for artists when using good paper is the term acid-free.

Traditionally the use of rosin during sizing meant that the rosin had to be adhered to the paper fibre with alum (an acidic compound). Paper made with this combination deteriorated in a relatively short time. Good-quality paper is now balanced to a neutral pH and is termed acid-free, and is used when archival stability is required.

Paper for water-based screenprint

Since paper absorbs water and the solvent for water-based ink is water, the type of paper used has to be carefully considered before printing. The degree to which a sheet of paper is affected by the ink is governed by a number of factors. Several years ago, at the Centre for Fine Print Research, we undertook a series of trials with the generous assistance of the Inveresk Paper Company, to try and find the best paper for water-based screen-printing. The results were unclear within the limited range of testing we were able to undertake, but proved that the problem was not as easily predictable as we imagined.

However, a few general commonsense rules apply, and please note these are general comments as all of these papers can be made to work with care and forethought. It is better to use a heavier weight of paper than you would for an oil-based ink. As a rule of thumb, papers of 200gsm and above are best. The best performing range of paper we tested tended to be the softer size sheets (by softer I mean with less size added into the sheet) with a NOT or HP surface. These papers seem to absorb the water and then dry out into their original shape and character. Paper with a hot-pressed surface that is heavily sized does not perform well. Once they have absorbed the water, they do not return easily to their original shape and surface. Waterleaf paper can perform well with some ink brands, in particular TW. Strangely, the cheapest papers such as newsprint perform extremely well with all brands. The reason for this was never ascertained.

The papers we use most tend to be mould-mades; for the majority of standard print jobs we use Somerset Satin 300gsm. Also good are German Etch 7317 285gsm, Arches Moulin de Gue 270gsm and Velin Arches Blanc 300gsm. If you want to print on a very lightweight sheet, some of the Japanese handmades work very well, such as Hodamura 245. These will absorb water very quickly and then flatten out as they dry. The Thai and Indian handmades, on the other hand, tend to absorb the moisture and then remain very cockled, as they dry without returning to their original shape. I also like using Arches 88 – for a waterleaf paper it performs very well. For a book grade we often print onto Zerkall 145gsm, though care has to be taken with these lighter weight papers. They are fine with a halftone or text, but they do not perform well with solids.

For general purpose educational use, we use a commercial grade high-speed blade card – Wiggins Teape 240 microns. This is heavy enough to

'Burn for love' by Renee Stout, USA. Colour screenprint with monotype on Arches 88 paper, ed. 50, 2000.
Printed by Dennis O Neil at Hand Print Workshop International, Alexandria Virginia, USA. Photo courtesy of Hand Print Workshop.

take the whole range of printing, with a smooth surface to make it easy to print on. Contrary to my previous comments, the surface seems not to absorb the water and remains fairly stable. This is probably because, due to the amount of additives in this type of paper, the water in the ink will have dried before it has time to penetrate the sheet.

Most handmade and mould-made papers have a front and a back. This is important as the front is the surface the manufacturer has designed all of the paper's surface characteristics into. The front is usually easily identified from a sheet's watermark. As the watermark will read correctly from the front, if no watermark exists, then it is often possible to tell from the deckle edge; the back of the deckle will lie perfectly flat while the front will show a rounded appearance, as the paper has seeped under the mould. On a mould-made sheet it is also possible to see a very straight line at the edge of the sheet before it becomes the deckle. On the back of a hand or mould-made sheet, it is usually possible to detect the marks of the weave in the mould the sheet was made upon.

Tearing paper

It is common practice to tear rather than cut a good sheet of paper to size. This should be done from the back of the sheet. First mark where you are going to tear, lay a heavy steel rule along the line to be torn and lift and tear the sheet against the edge of the ruler (see illustration). For a light-weight handmade sheet, it is customary to damp the edge before tearing.

Grain direction

Both mould-made and machine-made papers have a distinct grain direction. This is caused by the fibres being stretched and laid together as they land onto the moving belt of the machine. Handmade paper has no grain. The grain direction is referred to as short or long grain; long grain applies to following the direction of fibres, short grain refers to crossing the direction of the fibres at 90°.

The way to test for grain direction is to first lift the short edge of the sheet and try to gently fold it over onto itself, without creasing the sheet. Then try the same with the long edge of the sheet. The edge that shows the least resistance as you try and fold it over is parallel to the grain direction of the sheet. This is important for the manufacture of books, working out which way the sheet is going to stretch most whilst printing, and for knowing which way to roll prints when sending them in postal tubes (see Chapter Seven).

Above: tearing paper. Always tear from the back of the sheet.

Left: grain direction. Paper folds and bends easily along the grain – the left-hand sheet is against the grain and the right with the grain.

Handling paper

When handling paper, care should be taken to avoid denting the sheet. This occurs most with large sheets of paper. Dents show more when printed upon with solid colour. If handling large single sheets, the trick is to get air underneath the sheet and to try and float the sheet from place to place. If you need to move the sheet carefully and it is wet, pick it up by two opposite corners, let the middle of the sheet gently take its own weight and sag. The sheet can then be moved around the studio without it denting. With a pack of large sheets of paper, work out the grain direction, ease the pack over the edge of a bench with the grain direction parallel to the edge of the bench. When the pack is halfway off the bench, pick the pack up in the middle of the short grain edges, keeping the bend in the paper. If this is done with extreme care (see illustration), large sheets of paper can be moved without denting.

Above: handling paper. Pick up large sheets gently by two opposite corners to avoid dents.

Right: to carry packs of large paper, ease the pack from the table top with the grain running from right to left. Pick up and carry as shown.

Chapter 6

PRINTING

*This chapter covers mixing ink, preparing to print, registration,
printing, common problems, solutions to problems, cleaning the screen,
monoprinting with ink and with watercolour.*

Water-based ink, by its nature, is going to be cheaper to use than its solvent-based predecessors. Cleaning the screens and washing up with water has to be a saving over its solvent counterpart. In most cases, there is a further saving by not needing a large supply of rags. In most cases you can clean up by putting the screen in the sink and washing with water, or by using a sponge which can be rinsed frequently. However, further savings can also be made by treating the ink with a bit of forethought and maintaining good housekeeping.

Mixing ink

Remember the main ingredient of water-based ink is water. Therefore all the mixing receptacles have to be waterproof and non-metallic. The ideal mixing container is a small plastic cup or yoghurt pot, preferably with a sealable plastic lid. The majority of water-based inks seem to have a good shelf life if sealed from the air. All have a tendency to skin over and thicken if exposed to the atmosphere. Plastic mixing palette knives are preferable to metal as metal knives are prone to rust.

Quantities of base to pigment vary from ink type to ink type. It should be noted, as the mesh has a finer count when compared to solvent ink, a smaller amount will pass through the mesh. Therefore, in relative terms, you use less ink to cover the same area. The biggest saving we have made at the University of the West of England is in the size of mixing container

Using small ink pots can save vast amounts of waste.

71

we allow students. We only allow them to mix ink in 220ml (quarter pint) pots. This has nearly halved the ink bill compared to allowing them to use larger mixing containers. The cost of supplying these lidded containers is far outweighed by the gains made by reducing expenditure on inks throughout the year.

Surprisingly, water is the one item to avoid when mixing water-based inks. I recommended that if you need to thin your inks, try and use the manufacturer's recommended retarder. The majority of water-based inks require no thinning before use. The problem with water is that if it is mixed into the inks, it can have a tendency to attract bacteria. Once the water has attracted bacteria and started to stagnate, it will react badly with the ink by curdling it. When cleaning palette knifes, etc., try and clean them in a sink that has running water, not in a bucket that has been standing around. Likewise, clean all sponges and buckets frequently. Dry sponges out overnight rather than leaving them from day to day in a wet bucket. Also empty buckets out and leave them to dry out at the end of the day.

Registration

In industry this process is known as 'make ready' and follows a very set procedure. It is the process of setting up the screen and printing bed with the paper to be printed, to ensure that each colour is aligned correctly in relation to the paper edge and previous colours. For the printmaker it is good practice to follow these procedures. People often say, 'But is it worth it for just a few prints?'. The answer is always 'yes'.

The registration master
This is a sheet of the printing stock (paper) you are going to print on, that has been drawn up to indicate the following:

Where you want the image to print
The easiest solution is to attach the film positive or drafting film that you are about to print, in the correct position upon the registration master. It is now possible to register this accurately with the stencil on the screen.

To ensure that everything is printed in the correct place for the edition, I personally also tend to copy the original line drawing for my image onto a sheet of the same paper I will be using for printing (see Artwork preparation master line drawing). I then line this sheet up on top of the registration master sheet and use a pin to prick through the important areas that need to be registered accurately. These points are then drawn onto the registration sheet.

'Charts and Ciphers' by Allan Mann, Australia. Screenprint and letterpress, boxed folio book printed on Fabriano 5, 18 x 21cm, 1994.

Where the registration stops go

The purpose of the registration stops is to ensure that the image prints in exactly the same place on every sheet of paper and that each sheet of paper can be aligned with the next stencil in exactly the same position for printing the next colour. Determining where the registration stops go is normally fairly fixed as described below. There are however occasions such as when printing blends very long thin strips of solid, or long lines of type, where the positioning and direction of the stops is determined by the design.

Direction of pull

Direction of pull of the squeegee needs to be marked on the registration master sheet if very tight registration is called for, or a change of direction of pull may take place for design reasons and this has to be compensated for when registering the master sheet. The direction of printing should always be into the edge where the registration stops are situated.

Checking the machinery

This section is specifically written for hand-bench vacuum tables (see Chapter on Machinery) but the advice applies to all screenprinting.

Before locking the screen into the bed, first check that the bed is locked in position. Before fixing the screen in place, check that the stencil is the correct way round to match the registration master, and that the master sheet sits over the holes in the vacuum bed. The screen is then locked

PRINTING

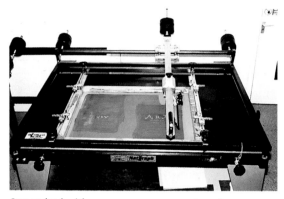

Screen bed with one arm squeegee set up for use. Note that the screen and bed have not been prepared for printing at this stage.

Off contact is the space between the top of the bonded vacuum top and the top frame. Distance is altered with threaded adjuster shown.

securely in place, so that it cannot move out of registration during printing. (See annotated illustration of vacuum bed on page 49.)

The off-contact or snap is then set at this point. Off-contact or snap being the gap between the underside of the screen and the surface of the print. This is partially set in relation to the following. What sort of image is being printed, how tight the screen is, how sharp the squeegee is and what the surface of the stock is, is partially a matter of choice and habit.

For a halftone or fine-detail image the snap is normally low (2 to 4mm ⅛ – ¼in.), for a large solid area it is usually higher in order to break the surface tension whilst printing (5 to 10mm/ ¼ – ⅜in.).

The tighter the screen, the lower the snap distance. The sharper the squeegee blade the lower the snap.

Registering the master

Once the screen is locked into place there are several methods of registering the master sheet on the bed of the press. Firstly, it is most common to attach the artwork from which the stencil was made to the master sheet. This can then be lined up with the stencil on the screen to ensure accurate registration (see illustration on p.75). The easiest method to line the sheet under the screen is by attaching a ruler to the sheet. It is then possible to manoeuvre the artwork whilst looking through the screen until the screen and the artwork are in register. The vacuum can then be turned on and the sheet registered with the acetate or PVC strips, more commonly referred to as stops or lays. Please note that though the screen and the artwork may appear to be in perfect register, once a print is taken, the pressure of the squeegee on the screen will stretch the screen sufficiently to move the print position in relation to the artwork below.

Above: registering though the screen with a ruler taped to the master sheet.

Above right: using an acetate registration sheet.

Right: fixing the stops made from soft PVC with double-sided tape on the back.

Care must therefore be taken to compensate for this when registering, if a very detailed halftone is being printed, or an extremely accurate fit is needed.

The other alternative is to lay up the master sheet on the bed of the press in approximately the correct position, then tightly tape a sheet of acetate in place on top (see illustration above). The acetate or PVC sheet must be clean, flat and unmarked. Check that the sheet is larger than the area to be printed and the screen will only print onto the acetate. Take a print then adjust the master sheet underneath until a perfect register is made. Fix the registration stops (see Fixing the stops, below) and remove the acetate sheet. This is the most accurate method of registration. Its downfall lies in the time necessary to register the print with the screen still flooded and drying. This is not a problem with the acrylic paint brands of ink such as Daler-Rowney and Lascaux, but can be a crucial factor for some of the other brands. Therefore it may be necessary to clean down the screen after printing the acetate.

Fixing the stops

This is the most important means of ensuring accurate registration. The stops should ideally be made of a soft PVC with double-sided tape on the back, though acetate or other forms of plastic are adequate. PVC is preferred in order to avoid breaking down the stencil on a long run. At a push, masking tape or card can be used, but these tend to deteriorate rapidly and are less accurate when printing longer runs. First, temporarily fix the registration sheet to the bed. Then stick to the bed of the press two stops (each approximately 4 x 2cm/1½ x ¾in.) in one of the facing corners, usually determined by whether the printer is left- or right-handed, at right angles to each other (see illustration on p. 75). A third stop should be positioned at the opposite end of the facing edge. Every sheet of paper is then fed in during printing to but up against these three stops, ensuring the image falls into the same place in relation to its position on the paper for every sheet printed. Some authorities recommend this third stop should be only two-thirds of the way down the sheet. This is acceptable if the stop is guaranteed to be fixed in the same place for every printing, or one is certain the sheet has been very accurately guillotined; otherwise placing the stop at the end automatically makes sure that it will fall in the same place every time, thus ensuring more accurate registration. If possible, the lay up of the print and the print order should be determined so that the facing edge is the longest edge of the paper stock. This factor will also assist in more accurate registration. Make sure with all prints that the paper is accurately placed against the stops, otherwise the effort of registration is pointless.

Masking and checking

If using a vacuum table it is very important to make sure all the holes that are not covered by the sheet you are printing are masked out. Otherwise you have not created the vacuum necessary in order to hold the sheet tightly in place whilst printing and consequently there is little point in using the vacuum table. A good suction can solve many of the problems associated with printing. Many of the common problems such as bleed or furry edges to a printing can be traced to poor adhesion of the paper to the bed, caused by the surface tension of the ink whilst printing. If I am printing a run of more than 50, I will also ensure that all of the masking paper is firmly taped to the bed approximately 1cm (½– ⅓in.)away from the paper on which I am printing. This means that the printing run can take place without tearing up or having to replace the masking paper, or constantly trying to maintain the vacuum suction.

Masking the vacuum bed. Note all the holes are covered with sheets of newsprint leaving only a 1cm gap around the print.

Taping the screen

If the screen has been made with several stencils exposed at the same time, those stencils not being printed need temporary masking to avoid ink bleeding through whilst printing the current stencil. This is normally achieved with plastic parcel tape (see Chapter 3). If the stencil to be blocked has been printed and you are confident it is not needed again it can be blocked with a screen filler.

Squeegees

The primary function of a squeegee is to force ink through the screen mesh in an even, constant film across the whole surface of the stencil.

Given the above, the importance of a sharp squeegee that is straight is paramount. It should not have any nicks or marks as these will create a physical printed line across the image. Nor should it have a wavy appearance, caused by it not being properly attached to the handle. The blade should have a sharp crisp edge with no signs of rounding.

Squeegees for hand-printing are usually either wooden or metal. Which you use is purely a matter of preference and comfort. The blade on the other hand is far more important. In industrial use, the squeegee blade has undergone major changes in the last ten years. Nearly all squeegee blades are now manufactured from urethane and are colour coded in relation to how hard it is. This hardness is referred to as *shore* or *durometer*. The range for screenprinting starts at 55 to 60 which is the softest through to 97 to 99 being the hardest. The standard for most artists' use is a shore of 70 to 75 and is usually green.

Squeegee blades come in a number of profiles and types. Artists use the standard rectangular section predominantly. Within this standard, a variety of types are available including double or triple shore which are laminations of differing hardness. The types are standard double or triple

Above: a typical squeege.

Left: squeegee blades of varying durometer.

shore, or hard blades with softer heads. All these types are for particular industrial uses, but if an artist is particularly heavy-handed or has difficulty getting enough pressure to print large areas, some of the triple shore squeegees with nylon cores and soft shore edges can be useful.

Printing

First, remove the registration sheet and lay a sheet of paper to be printed in place upon the vacuum table. Then turn on the vacuum and lower the screen. Remember the first sheet you print will not be quite the same colour or density as all the subsequent sheets.

Lay a line of ink about 2.5cm (1in.) wide in front of the stencil to be printed on the screen with the colour to be printed. Be fairly generous and make sure the puddle of ink is wider than the stencil. With the squeegee, flood the screen with ink by pushing the squeegee away from you, whilst holding the screen clear of the printing bed. This is normally done at a low angle with a gentle pressure to give a generous coat. The angle and pressure of flood will vary dependent on ink make and the style of the ink. Remember that this coat will dictate what is to happen when you print. The actual pull of the blade transfers what you deposited when you flooded the screen. This is particularly important to remember if printing blends. The reason for the flood coat is to deposit an even coating of ink into the mesh so that when you print, it is that even deposit which is laid on the paper.

This is one of the most important facts to remember in order to aid good printing. What you see in the screen when flooded is what it will look like on the paper. If you can spot any blemishes, do not print. You will then save throwing a print away.

When the stencil is flooded transfer the squeegee to behind the puddle of ink. Hold the squeegee so that your hands are in from each edge about half of the total distance remaining between your two hands on the squeegee. Your fingers should be spread out across the back edge of the squeegee above the blade. Press firmly and pull the squeegee towards you keeping it at an angle of about 60°. Pressure should come through your arms and fingers. Your thumbs should be used to maintain the correct angle. Do not exert too much pressure; bending the squeegee blade will cause the stencil to bleed. The aim is for a single point of contact between the edge of the blade, the screen and the paper. Pull over and past the image, but do not come too near the edge of the screen, as leaving pools of ink near the frame makes cleaning up much harder. Once you have reached the end of the pull, push the blade away from you slightly to leave a clean puddle of ink, lift the squeegee up and over the puddle of ink; if you have pushed it slightly away from the ink it will lift cleanly and not drip ink. Place the squeegee at the same angle as you pulled the print in

1. Putting on the ink.

2. Printing: starting the stroke.

3. Printing: note – try not to change the angle of the blade during printing.

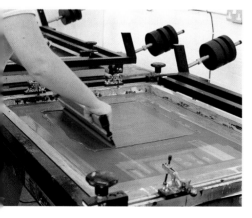

4. Finishing the pull.

5. Refreshing ink after printing and flooding.

front of the puddle (60° – the top of the handle facing towards you) then flood back. Again, do not push the puddle close to the edge of the frame. Pull the squeegee slightly back from the ink, lift it over the ink and rest it against the back of the screen. Some people turn the squeegee away from them in order to flood the screen. This coats both sides of the squeegee blade and can cause problems when priting a long run. The above mentioned means you are only using the front face and the blade of the squeegee. Ink is therefore refreshed constantly on the surface of the blade.

Lift the screen, take out and inspect the first sheet you have printed, check the register, colour and for any bleeds or pinholes in the stencil. If the sheet looks good, place it in the drying rack; then repeat the above sequence until you have printed the run. For long runs or with quick drying inks, it is useful to get a friend to rack the prints for you.

Trouble shooting

The most common problem encountered is the stencil bleeding around the edges. Why it happens is due to the surface tension being broken in the line of ink when you are printing. The ideal is for a single line of ink to have minimum contact at the point where the squeegee, the screen and the paper touch. Once the surface tension is broken, the ink can flood underneath the stencil, causing bleeds and fuzziness to the edges of the stencil. The most common causes are:

Screen too slack. The screen itself is able to contact too great an area of paper causing the ink to flow underneath. If it is only a little slack, the remedy is to increase the snap distance thus stretching the screen tighter. This can also throw the registration out. If the screen is very slack , the only option is to make a new stencil on a tight screen.

Squeegee too blunt. Too round an edge can cause the squeegee to cover too large a surface area. The remedy: use a sharper squeegee.

Not enough vacuum. This causes the paper to temporarily stick to the screen. The remedy: make sure all the exposed holes outside the paper size are blocked in the bed.

Ink too dilute. The ink is too thin to remain on the surface and tends to flow through the mesh. The remedy: try re-mixing the ink to a thicker consistency, or wait for it to dry on the screen for a while.

Build up of paper fluff or dry ink. If the stencil has bled frequently, an ink residue can build up on the back of the screen around the edge of the stencil. This in turn can cause further bleeding as it can interfere with the good contact between the screen and the paper. The same effect can occur on a very long run, as paper fluff builds up on the back of the stencil;

especially if a small amount of bleeding has occurred. This is most noticeable with very soft paper. Remedy: carefully clean the stencil on the back of the screen and make sure it is thoroughly dried.

Pressing too hard. This causes the squeegee blade to bend over, thus making too great a contact between the screen and the paper, allowing the ink to flood through the screen (see p. 79). Remedy: to press less hard, or if that then causes the image to not print, lower the snap and use a harder squeegee.

Too little snap. Very occasionally this can cause bleeding if the screen is almost in contact with the paper and does not have enough space to pull away from the paper after printing. Remedy: increase the snap.

Increasing the squeegee angle at the end of the stroke. It is natural as you pull the squeegee towards you to increase the angle. If it gets too steep it can squeeze the ink under the front of the stencil. Remedy: concentrate on printing at a constant angle.

Another common problem usually occurs when printing large solids, this is an inverted U-shape mark, often with small bubbles at the edges. It is caused by the paper having too much contact with the screen and a number of factors will contribute to it occurring:

Ink too thick. This causes the paper to stick to the underside of the screen. Remedy: thin the ink.

Screen too slack. Same effect as above. Remedy: raise the snap.

Vacuum too weak. This causes the paper to lift up and stick completely to the underside of the screen. If this partially happens, the sheet will commonly fall back out of register. Remedy: make sure all the holes are masked out. If this does not cure the problem, check that the holes in the bed are not blocked.

Uneven striped colouring in a solid can be caused by a squeegee which is no longer flat across its surface. Visually it is usually easy to tell if this is the case by looking along the blade. If it is not flat and level, change the blade.

Image does not print at the edges or does not print in parts. The causes of this can be many. Experience shows that visually most of the common causes can be differentiated.

Too much snap. This is recognised by the edges of the squeegee not being able to touch the paper, so only the centre of the image will have printed in the direction you have pulled the squeegee. Remedy: lower the snap.

Stencil has dried in. This is where, over a series of prints, the image starts to dry in from the edges in the mesh. The problem is usually caused by taking too much time to print. The remedy is to either print faster or clean up and start again. Sometimes a very thick flood coating is enough to open the mesh again. Nearly always it pays to clean up completely and start again.

Stencil is clogged. This can be where old ink is still dried into the mesh and was not cleaned out properly when the screen was washed; or can be caused if the emulsion from coating the screen has not been properly washed out and a residue is remaining in the screen. This is usually characterised by a line around the edge of the image not printing. Remedy: the only thing to do here is to clean up and wash the screen thoroughly. Then check if it is still clogged; remake the screen if the clogging refuses to budge.

Cleaning the screen

There are two primary methods of cleaning ink from a screen after printing. They are differentiated by a number of workshop conditions and working methods. They are perhaps most easily described as cleaning up for a communal workshop and cleaning up for the individual artist with perhaps more limited facilities.

Cleaning up in a communal workshop

In these conditions screens are constantly recycled, often on a more than daily basis, therefore the condition and cleanliness of the screen is

Above: cleaning the screen with a plastic palette knife.

Right: washing down the screen with water, after printing, to remove the ink.

paramount. With this in mind, the recommendation is to clean the screen by first scraping up the excess ink with a plastic (please note *plastic* – a metal blade will tear the screen) and returning it to the pot from which it came. Then remove the whole screen from the frame and take it to the wash room where it is hosed down with a gentle, not fierce, spray from a sprayer attached to the ordinary water supply. The screen is then dried.

The advantages of this system are: no rag or cleaning cloth is used and the screens suffer very little staining as the ink residue is washed away thoroughly and quickly; likewise the screens do not get clogged as any residue is washed out.

The disadvantages of this system are that it is difficult to change colour easily if you have mixed the wrong colour without having to dry and re-register the screen. Likewise, if a series of stencils is on the same screen that use the same registration, it can be frustrating to have to keep re-registering and drying the screen.

Cleaning up as an individual artist

In my workshop I have no running water and I like to proof and change a colour, perhaps five or six times, before I make a decision to run the edition. In these conditions it makes far more sense to leave the screen in register and clean it in situ. A bucket full of water and a sponge can be used for this, but bear in mind the problems of bacteria if using this method, and constantly change the water and wash the sponge frequently. I clean my screens up with a rag and a mild alkaline domestic cleaner. More care must be taken when using these products; a pair of rubber gloves is the only protection needed. The reason for using the mild alkali is it prevents the ink cross-linking with the acidic screen emulsion and hardening in the screen. It enables me to clean all the residue from the screen, thus reducing screen staining and preventing blocking.

The advantages of this system are: it is not necessary to have running water to hand. You do not have to break the registration in order to change colour.

The disadvantages to this system are: if not cleaned carefully, screens can become stained and clogged very quickly. Care must be taken in the use of mild alkalis. The cost is greater if alkali is used instead of water. This is not a problem. As an individual I estimate my increased costs per edition of prints to be in the order of £6 sterling ($10).

Monoprinting

Monoprinting is the technique of painting ink directly onto the screen without the use of a stencil. This gives a very immediate spontaneous result. Many artists use this process in preference to printing in the usual manner as they prefer the quality of mark achieved.

There are two types of monoprinting; painting onto the screen with ink then printing through the screen, or painting the screen with gouache or water colour, drying the screen, then printing the result.

Painting the screen with ink

This method is often the best means of quickly introducing new people to the screenprinting experience. At the same time it is a useful method of recycling unused ink. The preferred ink to use for this, from a practical point of view, are the acrylic brands with a screenprint medium specifically developed for artists' use (Daler Rowney, Lascaux, Golden, etc.). These inks all dry very slowly in the screen and with the addition of extra printing base can be slowed still further. It is possible to take an hour to paint the screen using one of these brands. If one uses an industrial brand such as Marler or TW, the monoprint has to be completed in a matter of minutes.

All that is necessary is a number of different coloured inks and a good supply of brushes to paint with. First, mask out a generous border around the edge of the screen. As in all other screenprinting, a border of at least 12.5cm/5in. all round is necessary. Prop the screen up away from the table surface. You can draw the initial design in pencil on the mesh, if required – these pencil marks will print. Use a soft pencil (2B or softer), as a hard pencil can damage the mesh. You can also place a drawing or photo underneath the screen to work from, as long as it does not touch the mesh while you are painting. Paint the monoprint on the inside of the screen. The only things to remember are that the first colour you paint on the screen will be most dominant, even if another colour is painted on top. It also does not matter if a fairly thick layer of ink builds up, as long as the whole printing surface of the screen is covered. (This avoids a splurge of unwanted colour in the areas not painted.) If an area is to remain unpainted, fill that area with transparent medium.

Drawing a monoprint using ink directly onto the screen and printing before it dries.

Painting a watercolour monoprint. First painted with watercolour paints and then dried before printing.

'Cherry pie' by Libby Lloyd, UK. Screenprint monoprint, 30 x 30cm, 1997.
Photo courtesy of the artist.

Once the screen has been painted, it is then locked into the printing
frame and a sheet of paper registered in place. Many people for this
method prefer to paint the screen locked and registered in situ. A line of
transparent printing medium is placed along the back of the screen in
preparation for printing. This helps to lubricate the pull of the squeegee.
A print is then pulled. The first print will be very strong in colour. If subsequent prints are pulled they will get progressively paler. Many people use
these subsequent prints as backgrounds for further monoprints. It may
seem to be stating the obvious, but pull your prints straight onto good
paper as you never know with monoprinting when you have got a good
print.

Most people treat monoprints of this type as a one-off experience
accepting or rejecting the resultant print after just one printing. Often
building up a set of prints adding parts to each print in a gradual build
up can yield quite different, very rich results. They can also be used in

PRINTING

combination with all the usual methods of printing such as paper stencils, photo imagery, etc.

Water colour and gouache monoprints

The delight of this method is that the cheaper the quality of water colour and gouache used the better the result. It is also a means of monoprinting which allows you lots of time to draw the image.

First work out what you are to draw and mask out a generous border around the edge of the screen. Again, a border of at least 12.5 cm (5 in.) all round is necessary. Then either place a drawing underneath the screen and trace the outline you need to work from, remembering that any pencil mark you make will print. Or prop the screen away from the drawing by about 1 cm (inches) and work from the drawing.

Paint with either gouache or watercolour; if you mix the two, remember that gouache, as it is a thicker medium with more opacity, has a tendency to block the screen. Watercolour will produce a more transparent effect. As with traditional watercolour you can either work wet in wet or build up the colour slowly, drying each before painting the next. If you use this method, as you paint, dry the screen with a hot air dryer, set on its coolest setting. It is very easy to overheat the screen, causing the mesh to break and ruining your work. When you have completed painting, make sure the screen is completely dry before trying to print. This is very important for the best effects.

When you are ready to print, lock the screen into the printing frame as normal, register the sheet to be printed onto the bed. Be aware that it is common to reprint the sheet several times with this technique, so registration is important. Place a line of transparent printing base in front of the area to be printed, then flood coat the screen and wait before you print. It is important that a thick flood coat takes place and that you wait with the screen flooded before printing. This waiting time is necessary to

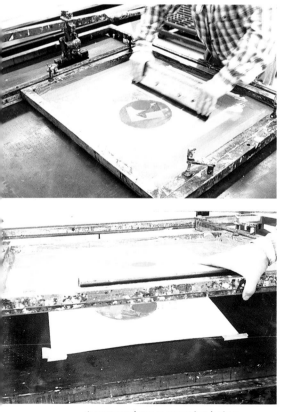

A watercolour monoprint being printed.

'I'm sure we could find one to fit you, chickpea suggested soothingly...'
by Gail Mason, UK. Watercolour monoprint, 55 x 76cm, 1998.
Photo permission the artist.

dissolve the dried watercolour in the screen. The time tends to vary between one to two minutes and
is dependent on the brand of printing medium used and the density of effect you wish to create. Once you pull a print it becomes visually clear why you wait; the result at its best is a delicate wash effect with a darker edge around each of the painted areas (see print by Gail Mason on the previous page). It may be necessary to pull the same print, in register, several times to achieve the desired density of colour. A number of prints may be pulled, but as in all monoprint techniques the successive prints become paler with each pull. For this technique these later prints are often good guides for drawing the next print or colour.

This is a very delicate technique that can be built up, not only slowly on the screen, but also through a number of different printings. Soft pencil, graphite sticks, charcoal and water-soluble colour pencils also work very well with this process. In my experience, it is advisable not to mix watercolour with gouache, primarily because they tend to dissolve at different rates in the screen. Therefore either the best watercolour effects are lost from over-absorption, or there is not enough time to dissolve the gouache in order to achieve the best watercolour effect

'London Jacket' (front) by Steve Mumberson, UK. Mixed media print, lifesize, 1998. Photo permission the artist.

Chapter 7

STUDIO SET-UP

*This chapter covers machinery, drying cabinets, vacuum beds,
pressure washers and exposure units plus proofing, editioning,
signing and keeping records.*

■ Machinery

The simplest form of screenprint
set up is a wooden screen hinged
to a baseboard and a squeegee (see
illustration). In the past it was
possible to function with just this
one piece of equipment. Now one
has to add a simple exposure unit
as well, and preferably a low-cost
pressure cleaning gun of the sort
used to clean cars. The screens can
be propped up in the dark and
dried with a fan heater. It is still
feasible with this simple equipment
to function from home at relatively
low cost.

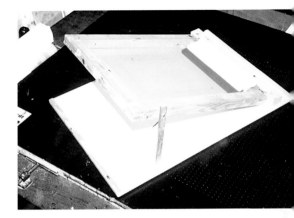

Wooden screen bed. This is the
simplest possible form of screen
printing.

Drying cabinets

One aspect of using direct coated emulsions is the need for a method of
drying screens in subdued or no light. This is fulfilled at least in the damp
conditions of the UK by a drying cabinet. These can take many forms but
the primary need is to dry screens horizontally so that the emulsion does
not slowly slide across and build up on one side of the screen.

Manufacturers of emulsion recommend drying the screens with the
emulsion side facing downwards. In theory this produces a better stencil
profile, due to the thin layer on the mesh side and more generous coat to
give better edge profile on the outside. In reality this is not a practical
solution; the emulsion sticks to whatever form of support the screen sits
on. The answer is to dry screens with the emulsion coat upwards. I have
never been into a printshop where this does not happen.

Drying cabinet with five sliding drawers. Wet screens are placed on the bottom (work upwards).

Drying cabinet. This cabinet has sliding bars to support the screens.

The best drying cabinet I have used was one made by Kippax and consisted of five drawers of approximately 15cm (6 in.) depth. Each drawer, which slid out on firm runners, had a sturdy wire mesh base, the drawers were surrounded with *small* to stop the light seeping in when closed and the dryer had a fan heater in the bottom which circulated the air which was vented at the top and rear of the cabinet. This design of dryer meant that assorted sizes of screens could be dried at the same time by laying them on the mesh to dry.

Other alternatives consist of adjustable bars on which the edges of the screens can be supported. These allow for greater flow of air, but suffer from the need to adjust the bars to accommodate differing screen sizes and the fact that screens can fall off the bars.

Pressure washers

I highly recommended that you use a pressure washer to clean your screens. These produce a fine spray at high pressure which will blast the screen clean. In the last five years these have become popular for domestic

Pressure washer.

use, to clean the car or garden path – so the price has dropped enormously. It is now possible to buy a washer of about 800 lb. pressure or above for around £100 ($60). The use of one of these washers will greatly reduce the amount of chemicals necessary to keep the screens clean. Once a stencil has been printed, the remaining ink residues and stencil can be cleaned from the screen with only a small amount of stencil remover. If used quickly after a colour has been printed they also greatly reduce screen-staining. Care must be taken to wear proper eye protection as these high pressures can be dangerous if not treated with care.

Vacuum tables (screen beds)

These come in a variety of types. Hand benches, semi automatic, parallel lift, but also differ greatly from country to county. In the UK nearly all hand benches have a fully adjustable floating vacuum top, whereas in the US this is rare. My ideal bed consists of a floating vacuum table, a hanging counterbalance weight system and a system of locking registration for the top frame. As very little published information is available on the pros and cons of vacuum tables for artists' use, the following is intended as a guide to aid selection. It is assumed the majority of artist-printmakers will still use a hand bench for printing.

Vacuum top

The surface of a vacuum table should be made of a plastic laminate; at one time aluminium alloy was used, but this tended to scratch easily. The holes should be drilled at 2 to 3 cm (¾ to1½in.) intervals with a generous allowance of non-print area. The construction of the top should be of a box construction with a honeycomb structure inside to maintain rigidity and allow the free passage of air through the top.

Points to check: Make sure the top is level with no depressions where extreme pressure has weakened the honeycomb structure. Check the surface has no scratches; deep scratches will show up on lightweight paper.

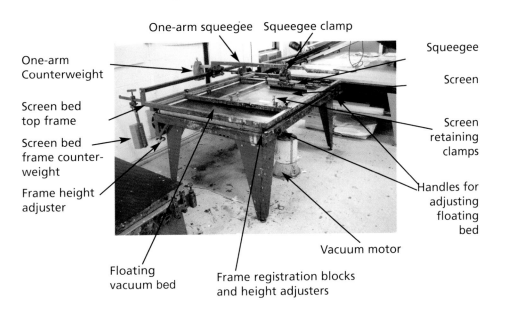

One-arm squeegee Squeegee clamp

One-arm Counterweight

Screen bed top frame

Screen bed frame counterweight

Frame height adjuster

Squeegee

Screen

Screen retaining clamps

Handles for adjusting floating bed

Vacuum motor

Floating vacuum bed

Frame registration blocks and height adjusters

Make sure all the holes are open and not blocked. If they have been drilled out to clean, check there is not a small raised lump around each hole caused by drilling, which will also show up on lightweight paper stock.

Suction

Test the vacuum with a large sheet of paper covering all the holes. The suction should be strong enough to make moving the sheet difficult when the screen has been lowered. Maintaining a strong vacuum is then a matter of masking the rest of the bed sufficiently if a small piece of paper is used. It is possible to buy quiet motors these days that create very little noise (see Suppliers List). Most vacuum tables in the UK use a sliding plate mechanism to turn the vacuum on and off thus avoiding the noise problems of the older solenoid systems.

Adjustment and registration

A floating bed is where the vacuum top sits on a series of pads above the frame of the table and is held in place with a series of springs and screw adjusters. There are normally three adjusters. One controls the movement from side to side, the other two are placed either side of the front of the table enabling front to back movement and a lateral twist. There is usually a means of locking the table in position once adjustment is complete.

Hinge mechanism

This needs to be considered carefully; it is the point of most tension and therefore needs to be of a robust nature. Any wear in this section can cause misregistration when printing. Check carefully, as some printing beds are manufactured with very sturdy tables and legs but have weak hinge mechanisms which will not stand the strain of long term printing.

Above: Hinge mechanism. This is the point of a vucuum bed that takes the most wear and tear – frequent maintanance is advised.

Left: Floating bed. Note the adjuster to move the whole of the vacuum top.

Weights: straight adjustable counter-balance.

Top Frame with adjustable insert bars to hold the screen. Note the hanging counterbalance.

Weights

These come in several forms; either as a straight counterbalance from the back of the bed, or as a hanging counterbalance which stops the frame from crashing as it reaches the top of its pivot. Some beds now have a countersprung mechanism underneath which balances the top frame. All are adjustable to allow the minimum of effort in order to lift and balance the top frame. The use of this adjustment is often neglected and if adjusted properly, even on a short run, can make printing a more pleasurable experience.

Top frame

It is generally accepted that a top frame is a better solution than just two individual arms. A rigid top frame, as long at it has a good system of internally adjustable arms, and is well integrated with the hinge mechanism, will give very accurate results. This system has the advantage of accepting a wide variety of screen sizes with very little adjustment.

Clamp mechanism

Within the top frame, in most cases, are two bars with flange plates on the base to support the screen. These are fully adjustable to accommodate any width of screen and can be clamped in position. On each bar is normally a pair of adjustable quick-release toggle clamps or in some instances a threaded clamp (see illustrations overleaf).

Off contact (snap adjustment)

This takes the form of two screw threads, one above each part of the hinge mechanism to raise and lower the back of the top frame. At the front of the top frame, each front leg normally has an adjustable screw thread to raise and lower the front. It is important that all these threads are in good working order. The adjustable screws at the front usually fit into some form of registration block to ensure stability of the whole top frame.

Clamp mechanism 1. This is the most comon type of toggle clamp.

Clamp mechanism 2. Putting weight on the back of this clamp whilst tightening makes fixing this type of clamp easier.

One arm squeegee – used to print large areas of colour, flooding the screen before printing.

One-arm squeegee

This is the metal arm attached to a vacuum bed for printing large areas of colour. A squeegee is clamped into the mechanism and it enables you to apply greater and more even pressure across the surface of the squeegee blade. To use one properly you need at least 20cm (8in.) of space between the edge of the stencil and the screen frame on each side. This allows you to print properly and transfer the squeegee over to the other side of the ink puddle.

When printing, place ink on the screen as normal and flood the screen with the arm. At the end of the flood, pull the squeegee slightly away from the puddle of ink and then lift the squeegee over the puddle, lay it at the opposite angle and print. Repeat the procedure as for the flood. A steep angle is required for the printing stroke, which should be towards the registration corner, and a much shallower angle is required for the flood stroke.

A few important points to remember:

• Use a squeegee that is at least 2.5cm (1in.) wider on each side than the stencil. With the pressure exerted when printing, the edges of the squeegee can drag. The effect caused is the edges do not print if the squeegee is not wider than normal.

• Balance the weights on the arm in conjunction with the counter-balance weights. The frame and squeegee should be balanced so it takes little effort to lift the screen, but the one arm should not feel heavy when lifting the squeegee over the ink at the end of each stroke. It is important to move the squeegee away from the puddle of ink at the end of each stroke to avoid dripping ink everywhere.

• Do not have too much ink on the screen at one time. Keep a small squeegee at the back of the frame and frequently gather up the ink which will travel to the back of the screen. Add more ink little and often.

• Remember, when printing very large areas of colour, if you are checking how the colour is printing with the paper still on the bed of the press, not to let the back of your head touch the ink in the stencil. Not only can you look very silly with bright coloured ink in your hair but more importantly, you can also ruin a print.

Exposure units

The simple form of exposure unit consists of a single mercury vapour lamp (usually 125 watt); a box to contain it in, a sheet of glass at the top of the box to lay the screen upon, and a means of blocking the light whilst the screen and stencil are positioned on top of the box. A manufactured sealed unit such as a Graphoscreen can be obtained, which is a more sophisticated version of the above description.

A separate light source and printing down frame is the most common means of exposing stencils. The light source is normally quartz halide and has a power between 1 and 5 kW. This form of lighting takes time to warm up and reach full strength, which means two things. Firstly the light source will be left on most of the time and have a shutter that opens and closes to expose the light to the screen. Many have a means of reducing the power whilst they are left in the idle position.

Secondly, as these light sources give differing amount of light, dependent on how warmed up they are and how long they have been in use. The exposure to the screen is calculated using an integrator. This is simply a photoelectric cell that measures the amount of light emitted from the lamp and calculates the exposure accordingly. It will calculate the exposure in a number of units based on light intensity, not on time. Therefore if an exposure is set on 30 units, this equates to the screen

Light source. This is a 1 kilowatt quartz halide light source.

Integrator. The small photo-electric cell is in the bottom left-hand corner.

receiving a specified amount of light in order to expose the stencil. In the morning that might be 6 minutes in time. If the lamp is cold in the afternoon that same amount of light might be emitted in 4 minutes if the lamp is warm. As long as the exposure is set at the same number of units it will receive the same amount of light

Provided of course that the distance of the lamp from the printing down frame is kept as a constant. Working out this distance, if there is not a set of manufacturers instructions available, can be a matter of trial and error. A good guideline is, if the full area of the frame is to be used, then the lamp should be placed at the same distance as the diagonal across the glass of the printing down frame. If the light is placed too near, then it will be concentrated on one spot and the edges of the stencil will be under-exposed. If too far away then the exposure times become too long and the stencil will still be poor. As a rule of thumb, if you double the distance of the lamp from the frame, then you need to quadruple the exposure time. Halving the distance requires one quarter of the exposure time.

If exposure times still prove to be problematic, most manufacturers of emulsions sell exposure calculators. From one exposure these calculate whether you are under or over-exposing and the sort of time changes necessary. Autotype, in the UK, make a very good calculator.

Printing down frames

The printing down frame consists of a large piece of plate glass fixed in a swivelling frame with a hinged top, covered with a flexible rubber sheet which, when used in connection with a vacuum pump, forces the screen and stencil into contact together against the plate glass top. The stencil is placed onto the glass. The screen, with its light-sensitive coating, is placed in contact against the stencil and the top with the rubber covering lowered to cover the screen and stencil and locked into place. The vacuum is then turned on and the air is pumped out between the glass and the blanket so that good contact is made between the glass, the stencil and the emulsion coating on the screen. The frame is then swung through 90° to the vertical so the stencil may be exposed to the light source.

Drying racks

The commonest method of drying prints is to use a rack fitted with welded wire trays held in place by springs, most commonly with 50 trays to a rack. Racks are the items that suffer most from abuse in studios. If piles of prints are stacked on individual trays, or they are lent on heavily by users, the trays will bend. The springs are also prone to wear. For best conditions to aid drying, a good circulation of air needs to pass evenly around all the prints in the rack. If the trays are bent or the springs fail, prints can easily be marked or damaged. This can cause much heartache if, after all the effort of printing, at the last minute your print is damaged in the rack. Treat racks with care and they will last many years. Be cautious and look carefully before buying if considering second-hand.

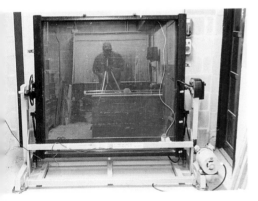

Above: Printing down frame.

Right: Drying rack. If care is taken several prints may be stacked to a tray when printing large editions.

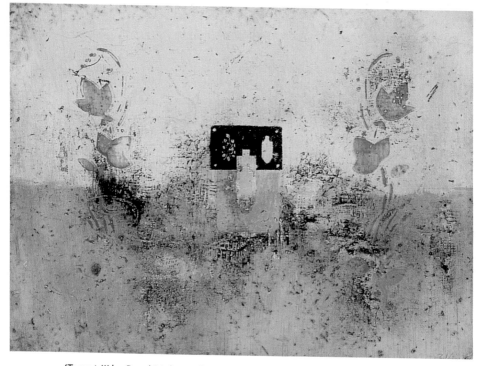

'Target II' by Pavel Makov, Ukraine. Screenprint on Arches 88 paper, 59 x 71cm, 1998, printed by Dennis O Neil at Hand Print Workshop International, Alexandria, Virginia, USA.
Photo courtesy of Hand Print Workshop.

Proofing, editioning and keeping records

In the past there tended to be two approaches to producing an edition of screenprints. These are primarily split between the methods of the studio system and the approach of the individual artist-printmaker.

The studios traditionally made all the stencils first, exposed a complete set of screens for all the printings, proofed perhaps 5 to 10 copies making all the colour changes and decisions along the way. Then only when the proof was complete and had been signed off by the artist, was the edition printed.

The artist-printmaker, on the other hand, usually made the stencils on the screen, one at a time, and proofed and editioned at one and the same time. Often this was due to the simple expediency of only owning a very few screens.

The reality for most people these days is somewhere between the two. Studios can no longer afford the luxury of a lengthy proofing stage, so tend to proof only two or three colours ahead of the edition. This means proofing two or three colours. Then if the artist is happy, the edition is printed to this stage, then a few of the prints are proofed with the next two or three colours, and the edition follows up two or three colours behind. Artists who print their own work do something similar, as this is the most economic method for producing an edition.

Several factors need to be taken into account if this method of proofing slightly ahead of the edition is to be used. Always keep the original artwork and the positives at hand until the edition is complete and signed off. You never know when you may need to go back and remake a stencil.

Wet colour samples. Pots of ink like these will keep for several months without drying out. Matching to these wet samples is much easier.

Keep a wet sample of all the colours you have mixed, not just the colour you decided to print in the end. Often when you are several colours down the line that colour which was not good enough for a previous trial would be perfect for the current printing. A wet sample is far easier to match when remixing colour than a dry piece of colour in the middle of a print. This is because you are not comparing the wet sample to other colours surrounding it and the paper is not influencing your decision.

When editioning, the rule of thumb to guide how many extra sheets of paper you start with is as follows. If you are used to printing, allow for losing two prints per colour or 10% of the total edition, whichever is the least number of sheets. If you are unsure of your printing skills or have not clarified your ideas as to what the print might look like then allow more than this.

Signing prints

The accepted standards governing signing editions are that all signing is carried out in pencil. The norm is to use a well-sharpened B pencil.

The print is numbered in the left-hand corner of the print, usually but not exclusively, just below the image and on the blank paper border around the print using the convention of the number of the print above the number of prints in the edition, thus $\frac{1}{20}$, $\frac{2}{20}$, $\frac{3}{20}$, etc. This denotes print numbers 1, 2 and 3 from an edition of 20 prints (overleaf).

The artist's signature appears parallel with the number of the edition on the right-hand side of the print. The title of the print is in the centre

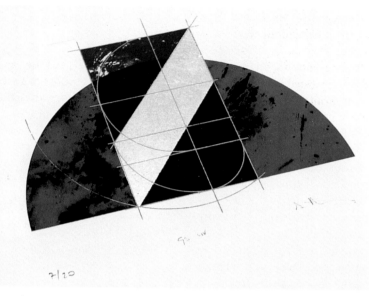

How to number and sign an edition of prints.

between the number and the artist's signature. Other acceptable notations used over and above the numbered edition are:

• A/P or artist's proof. This is accepted by common practice to be no more than 10% of the edition and by tradition are the copies owned by the artist when the edition has been commissioned by a publisher who is not the artist.

• BAT. Stands for *Bon à tirer*, French for good to go or good to run. This is the copy agreed by both the artist and the printer to be of a satisfactory standard to print. It is then used by the editioning studio to check the standard of the edition as it is printed.

• Printer's proof. Traditionally the copy signed by the artist and owned by the actual person who physically printed the edition.

• Studio proof. The copy signed by the artist for the studio archive.

• H/C. Stands for *Hors de Commerce*, not for sale. Often inferior standard copies used by the publisher to sell the edition from, so as not to damage any prints from the edition itself.

• State proof. Usually applies to etching and refers to an early version of an unfinished print.

• Insurance proofs. Very occasionally a publisher insists on extra copies which are not signed and can be used to replace damaged copies. This only happens with very large editions of, for example, 250+. The artist is usually asked to sign the replacement print and witness the damaged print being destroyed.

The convention with monoprints is not to number them as they are normally considered unique. In cases where an artist produces a set of monoprints where an attempt has been made to reproduce the same image, then the prints would be numbered as an edition.

Storage

Prints are best kept flat, in a plans chest or on shelves. Ideally they should be interleaved with acid-free tissue. Storage conditions should preferably be cool and dry. Avoid at all costs large changes of humidity, especially if prints are stored in plastic bags. Most artists store each edition sealed in plastic bags. Do not try and put too many prints in one bag.

It is important to keep good records of prints signed and sold. The advantage of screenprinting is that the whole edition is usually printed in one go. The problem occurs if it is not signed completely at the same time. Most artists I know, myself included, if they print the edition themselves, sign the prints as they are sold. This is only a problem if accurate records are not kept as to what number in the edition has been reached. It also pays to keep control over where prints have been sent and who they have been sent to. The advantage of multiple copies means that prints can be on exhibition or loan to several venues. In the case of the International Print Biennales this means you may not see a copy of a print for several years.

The beauty of being a printmaker is you have more than one copy of a print. Therefore the ability to post prints around the world is one of the perks attached to the job.

When rolling prints for postage, use a tube of a minimum 10cm (4in.) diameter. Roll all prints parallel to the grain direction of the paper. Roll with the image facing inwards, interleaf prints with tissue. Roll to a size slightly smaller than the inside diameter of the tube. Wrap the outside of the prints in tissue paper, secure the tissue to itself with tape and fold the ends of the tissue into the roll of prints. The prints should now slide easily in and out of the tube. Pack the ends of the tube with tissue so the prints are secure, and seal the end caps with plastic parcel tape to keep moisture out. If receiving prints that have been rolled, take them out of the tube and let them rest for a while, then put under weight for a couple of days before storing flat.

Happy printing, and may your prints be selected for many print exhibitions throughout the world.

'*And kissed him*' by Marcus Rees Roberts, UK.
Photo courtesy Pratt Contemporary Art, Kent , UK.

GLOSSARY

Adobe Photoshop
The industry standard computer image and photographic manipulation software

Amberlith/Rubylith
Knife cut masking films for creating stencils

Chinagraph
Grease based pencil, commonly sold for marking glass, used for drawing masks on film to make stencils

CMYK
Refers to the halftone four colour separation system. Cyan, Magenta, Yellow and Keyline (Black)

Coating trough
Shallow trough used for coating screens with direct emulsions

Colour separations
The individual stencils which when printed together create all the colours

Cockling
Cockling refers to the expansion that takes place when a sheet of paper gets damp, the sheet no longer lies flat and takes on a wavy appearance. Sometimes referred to as buckling.

Direct emulsion
Light sensitive emulsion in liquid form coated onto a screen, exposed and then developed in water to form a stencil

Direct/indirect
Light sensitive emulsion coated onto a plastic backing which may be attached to the screen then exposed or exposed first, washed out and then attached to the screen to form a stencil

Dpi
Dots per inch the system of apportioning tone used by computers as a default. dpi dots are of a uniform size and tone is expressed by the distance between the dots

Drafting film
Polyester film used for drawing stencils, traditionally smooth and matt and known under the trade name of Kodatrace or Permatrace. The new generation is textured and known as True-grain, Lexan or Mark resist

Drying in
Drying in refers to the process of the ink drying around the edges of the open stencil (image)areas of the screen. This results in crisply printed edges taking on on a furry or feathered appearance and resulting in a loss of detail

Drying rack
A movable set of wire trays used for drying prints

Exposure unit
A combined light source and printing down frame used to expose stencils onto screens

Floating bed
A table top vacuum area which has adjusters to move the top independently from the screen frame

Halftone
A means of creating artificial tone through a dot structure in order to render tonal ranges that are capable of being printed, measured in Lines per Inch

Hand bench
Generic name for a hand operated screenprinting table

High modulus screens
Extremely tightly stretched screens, approx. 40 Newton's rather than the normal 14. Used in industry to create extremely accurate registration

Indirect stencils
Light sensitive stencils with a polyester backing that are exposed and washed out first before applying them wet to the screen. When dry the polyester backing is peeled away.

Integrator
A photo-electric cell which reads the amount of light generated from a light source and used to guarantee that each exposure receives exactly the same amount of light

Kodatrace
See drafting films

Knife cut films
See Amberlith/Rubylith

Laser films
Polyester translucent films created specially for use with thermal laser printers to obtain low cost photographic stencils

Lexan
See drafting films

Light source
Name given to the Ultraviolet light used to expose the screen stencils

Lpi
Unit of measurement used for halftones and refers to the number of lines necessary to form a grid corresponding to the number of dots in the halftone

Mark Resist
See drafting films

Medium
The printing base into which colour is added

Mesh
The monofilament polyester mesh stretched over a frame is known as the mesh

Microns
The measurement used to gauge the thickness of a sheet of paper

Moiré
An interference pattern caused by the dot structure of a halftone clashing with the weave of the mesh causing an effect similar to watered silk

Monoprint
A one off print, usually created by directly painting ink onto the screen in some form

Mr Muscle
A mild alkaline household cleaner used to neutralise the acidity of the screen emulsion whilst printing, any mild alkaline may be used

One arm
The mechanism used for holding wide squeegees, enabling greater pressure to be exerted, so that a larger area may be evenly printed.

Photopaque
Photopaque refers to a red coloured gouache material traditionally used for spotting negatives in reprographics

Photopolymer emulsions
The generic name for all light sensitive screen emulsions

Pressure washer
Sometimes referred to as a Hydroblitz, this is a high pressure water spray for cleaning screens

Printing down frame
The vacuum frame that holds screen and stencil in close contact whilst exposure to ultra violet light takes place

Prosterisation
The production of several positives of varying densities from one black and white negative (usually one under exposed, one normal density, one over exposed). When printed this leads to the appearance of more solid rendering

Quartz Halide light sources
High powered light sources emitting ultra violet light

Quark Xpress
The industry standard computer publishing programme

Retarder
Used to slow (retard) the drying time of an ink

RGB colour
The colour system based on light, Red, Green and Blue used when scanning into a computer. This is converted to CMYK for output

Scanning
The process of capturing a picture to create a digital computer file

Screen
The frame and mesh used for holding the stencil

Shore/durometer
The measurement used to describe the hardness of a squeegee blade. The higher the number the harder the squeegee blade

Snap
The distance between the underside of the screen and the printing surface, snap means only the edge of the squeegee is in contact with the paper , thus avoiding problems of surface tension

Squeegee
The wooden or metal handle which contains the urethane printing blade

Stencil
Can refer either to the piece of artwork from which the stencil on the screen is created or to the stencil itself on the screen

Textured films
See drafting film

True Grain
See drafting films

Vacuum bed
Generic name given to a Hand printing screen bench, also can refer just to the table top suction area

'Dream Building (Gold)' by William Christenberry, US. Colour screenprint with monotype, ed. 57, published 2000. Printed by Dennis O Neil at Hand Print Workshop International, Alexandria, Virginia, US.
Photo courtesy of Hand Print Workshop.

LIST OF SUPPLIERS

UK

Paper

R. K. Burt
57 Union Street
London SE1
Tel: 020 7407 6474
Supplier of paper for artists

Falkiner Fine Papers
76 Southampton Row
London WC1
Tel: 020 78311151
Supplier of paper for artists

John Purcell Paper
15 Rumsey Road
London SW9 OTR
Tel: 020 77375199
Supplier of paper for artists, plus TW inks and True grain drawing films

Whatman International Ltd
Springfield Mill
Maidstone
Kent ME14 2LE
Tel: 01622 670755
Suppliers of printmaking and watercolour papers

Ink

Ash coatings
Shepherds Grove Industrial Estate
Stanton
Sussex IP31 2AR
Suppliers of Aqualex Inks

J. W. Bollom & Co
(J. T. Keep and Sons)
PO. Box 78
Croyden Road
Elmers End
Beckenham
Kent BR3 4BL
Suppliers of Sinvaqua inks and other screenprint supplies

Coates Lorrileux
Cray Avenue
St Mary Cray
Orpington
Kent BR5 3PP
Suppliers of Hydroprint inks and other screenprint supplies

Daler-Rowney Ltd
PO. Box 10
Bracknell
Berkshire RG12 8ST
Tel: 01344 424621
Suppliers of System 3 Acrylic inks and general art materials

A. P. Fitzpatrick,
142 Cambridge Heath Road,
London E1 5QJ
Tel: 020 7790 0884
Suppliers of Lascaux Studio and Gouache inks and other general art supplies

Gibbon Inks and Coatings
14-22 Coleman Fields
London N1 7AE
Tel: 020 7354 4246
Suppliers of Marler Paintbox and other screenprint supplies

John Purcell Paper
15 Rumsey Road
London SW9 OTR
Tel: 020 7737 5199
Suppliers of TW inks and specialist artist's paper

T. N. Lawrence (mail order)
208 Portland Road
Hove, BN3 5QT
Tel: 01273 260260
Suppliers of Hunts Speedball inks and other specialist printmaking supplies

Small Products
20 St. Andrews Way,
off Devons Road, Bow,
London E3 3PA
Suppliers of Aquagraphic Inks

General Screenprint Supplies

R. B. Graphics
2a Gadway House
Leigh Street
High Wycombe
Bucks HP11 2QU
Tel: 01494 441969
*Screenprint supplies for artist printmakers
including Mark Resist drawing film,
plastic mixing pots, plastic spatulas etc.*

Gibbon Inks and Coatings
14-22 Coleman Fields
London N1 7AE
Tel 020 7354 4246
*Suppliers of Folex emulsions, Safeguard
cleaning products plus Aquafill water
resistant green filler*

Sericol
Westwood Road
Broadstairs
Kent CT10 2PA
Largest commercial screenprint suppliers

VT Plastics
Unit 24
The Fort Industrial Park
Chester Road
Birmingham B35 7AR
*Suppliers of Kissel and Wolf including all
Pregan products and coating troughs*

Machinery

Fox Graphic Machinery
KG House
Kingsfield Close
Gladstone Industry
Dallington
Northampton NN5 7QS
*New and secondhand hand benches, racks,
exposure units and all machinery*

H.G. Kippax
Upper Bankfield Mills
Almondsbury Bank
Huddersfield HD5 8HF
*Hand benches, racks, exposure units
and all machinery*

Richards of Hull
Unit 1, Acorn Industrial Estate
Hull
Tel: 01482 442422
Screenprint washing troughs and sinks

Natgraph Ltd
Dabell Avenue
Blenheim Industrial Estate
Nottingham NG6 8WA
*Hand benches, racks, exposure units
and all machinery*

Trumax Ltd
Tower Road
Warmley
Bristol BS15 2XL
*Hand benches, racks, exposure units
and all machinery*

Screens

Tick Tack Ltd
Unit 15
Lawrence Hill Industrial Park
Croyden Street
Bristol BS5
Tel: 0117 954 1101
Will deliver nationally on larger orders

Coated Screens Ltd
Orchard House, Church Lane
Wallington
Surrey SM6 7ND
Tel: 020 8773 2331

Emulsions

Autotype International Ltd
Grove Road
Wantage
Oxfordshire X12 7BZ
*Overseas supplies only. All Autotype
emulsions supplied through Sericol
in the UK*

VT Plastics
Unit 24
The Fort Industrial Park
Chester Road
Birmingham B35 7AR
*Suppliers of Kissel and Wolf including all
Pregan products and coating troughs*

Laser print Films and other graphic art supplies

Folex
18-19 Monkspath Business Park
Shirley
Solihull
West Midlands B40 9NY

USA

Paper

A.N.W. Crestwood
205 Chubb Avenue
Lyndhurst
NJ 07071
Tel: +201 438 6869

Legion Paper
11 Madison Avenue
New York, NY 10010
Tel: +212 683 6990
Extensive range of Printmaking Papers

Ledion Paper West
6333 Chalet Drive
Los Angeles
CA 90040
Tel: +562 928 5600

New York Central Art Supplies
62 3rd St
NY 10003
Tel: +212 477 0400

Steiner Paper Corp.
145 40th St
Irvington
NJ 07111
Tel: +973 373 4279

Ink

Daler-Rowney USA
2 Corporate Drive
Cranbury
NJ 08512 9584
Tel: +609 655 5252
Suppliers of System 3 Acrylics

Hunt Manufacturing Co.
Statesville, NC 28677
Manufactures of Speedball inks

Pearl Paint (branches
throughout America)
308 Canal Street
New York 100113
*Stock Golden Acrylic inks and
general art supplies*

TW Graphics
7220 East Slausen Avenue
City of Commerce
Los Angeles
CA 900 40
Tel: +818 344 6663
*Manufactures of TW graphics inks
and all screenprint supplies*

Union Ink company Inc
463 Broad Avenue
Ridgefield
NJ 07657
*Manufacturers of Union ink and all
screenprint supplies*

Emulsions

Autotype Americas Inc
2050 Hammond Drive
Schaumburg
Il 60173
Tel: 1 800 232 0632
*All types of Photo emulsions
and masking films*

Ulano Corporation
255 Butler Street
Brooklyn
NY 11217
*All types of Photo emulsion
and masking film*

Mail order supplies

Dick Blick Art Materials
PO Box 1267
Galesburg
IL 61402 1267
Tel: 1 800 447 8192
*Stock: Hunts Speedball, Nasdar and own
brand inks, Paper plus general screenprint
supplies*

Daniel Smith Inc
4130 1st Street South
Seattle
Washington 98134
Tel: +206 223 9599
*Suppliers of specialist printmaking
materials and Speedball inks*

BIBLIOGRAPHY

Carey, Francis and Griffiths, Anthony. *Avant Garde British Printmaking* 1914–1960. The Trustees of the British Museum, 1990. ISBN 0 7141 1646 7

Castleman, *Riva Prints of the 20th Century.* Thames & Hudson. 1988. ISBN 0 500 20228 1

Gilmour, Pat, *Ken Tyler Master Printer.* Australian National Gallery & Hudson Hill Press, 1986. ISBN 0 9339 2016 4

Gilmour, Pat, *The Mechanised Image.* Arts Council of Great Britain, 1978. ISBN 0 7287 0156 1

Hanson, Trudy, V. Mickenburg, David, Moser, Joann, and Walker, Barry, *Printmaking in America Collaborative Prints and Presses.* Harry N. Abrams Inc., 1995 ISBN 0 8109 3743 3

Hening, Roni, *Water-based Screenprinting*, Watson Guptill, 1994. ISBN 0 8230 5644 9

Ivins, William M., *Prints and Visual Communication.* Routledge and Kegan Paul Ltd, 1953

Krill, John, *English Artists Paper.* Trefoil Publications, 1987. ISBN 0 8629 4093 1

Mara, Tim, *Screenprinting.* Thames & Hudson, 1979.

Peyskens, Andre, *The Technical Fundamentals of Screen making.* SAATI S.p.a. Screen-printing division, Como, Italy, 1989.

Scott, Paul, *Ceramics and Print.* A & C Black, 1994. ISBN 0 7136 3746 3

Stephens, John, *Screen Process Printing.* Blueprint, 1987. Second edition 1996

Saff, Donald and Sacilotto, Deli. *Printmaking History and Process.* Holt, Reinhart and Winston Inc., 1978. ISBN 0 0308 5663 9

Tallman, Susan, *The Contemporary Print from Pre-pop to Postmodern.* Thames & Hudson, 1996. ISBN 0 500 23684 4

The Technical Section of the British Paper and Board Makers' Association, *Paper Making; a general account of its history, processes and applications,* 1950.

INDEX